NEWSLETTER BONUS

Sign up to our free newsletter at **ColorfulCalm.com**

You will receive free coloring pages, information on our latest book releases, as well as a chance to win free coloring supplies.

Thank you for purchasing "Funny Swear Words (And Insults) From Around The World!"

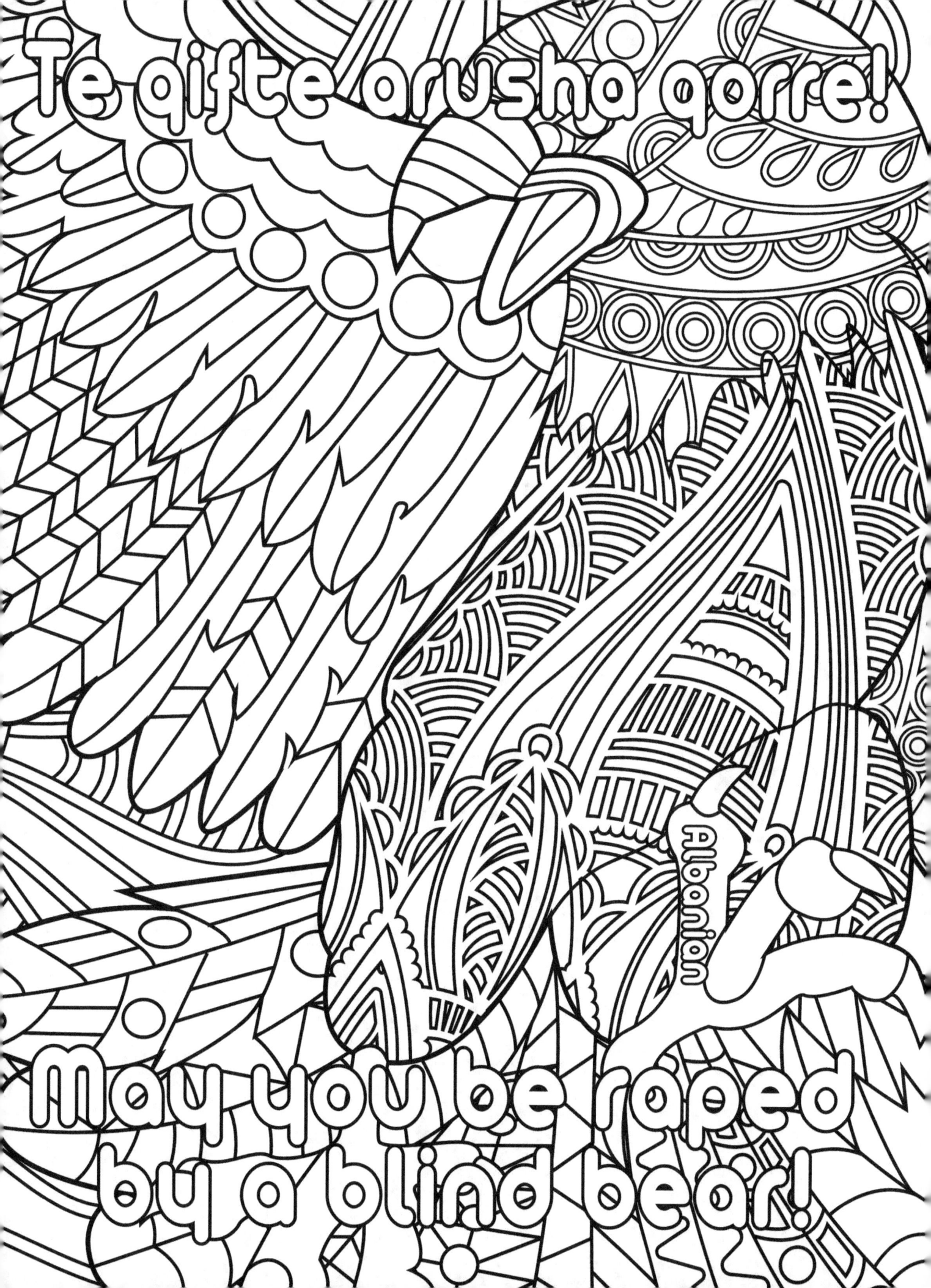

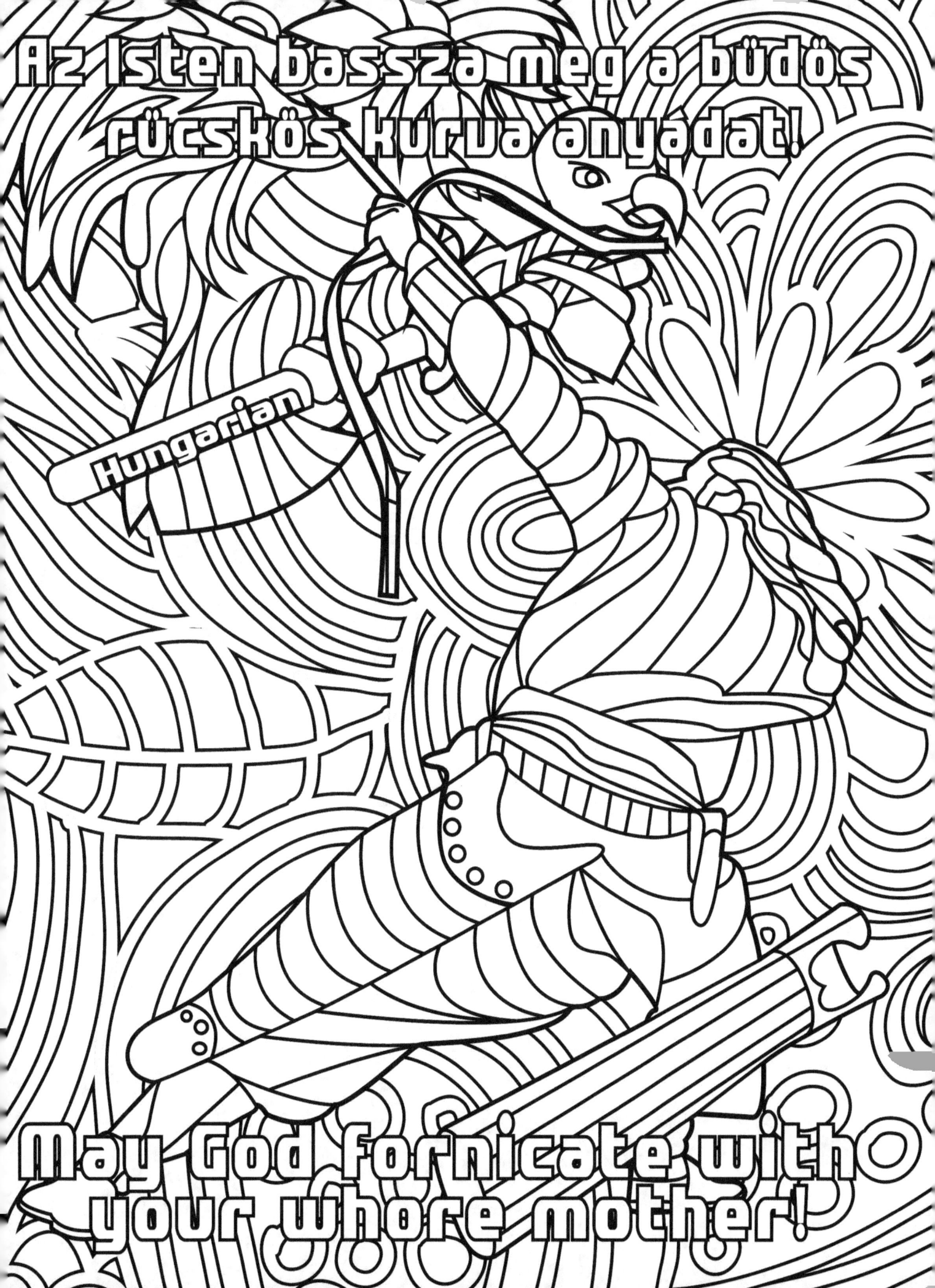

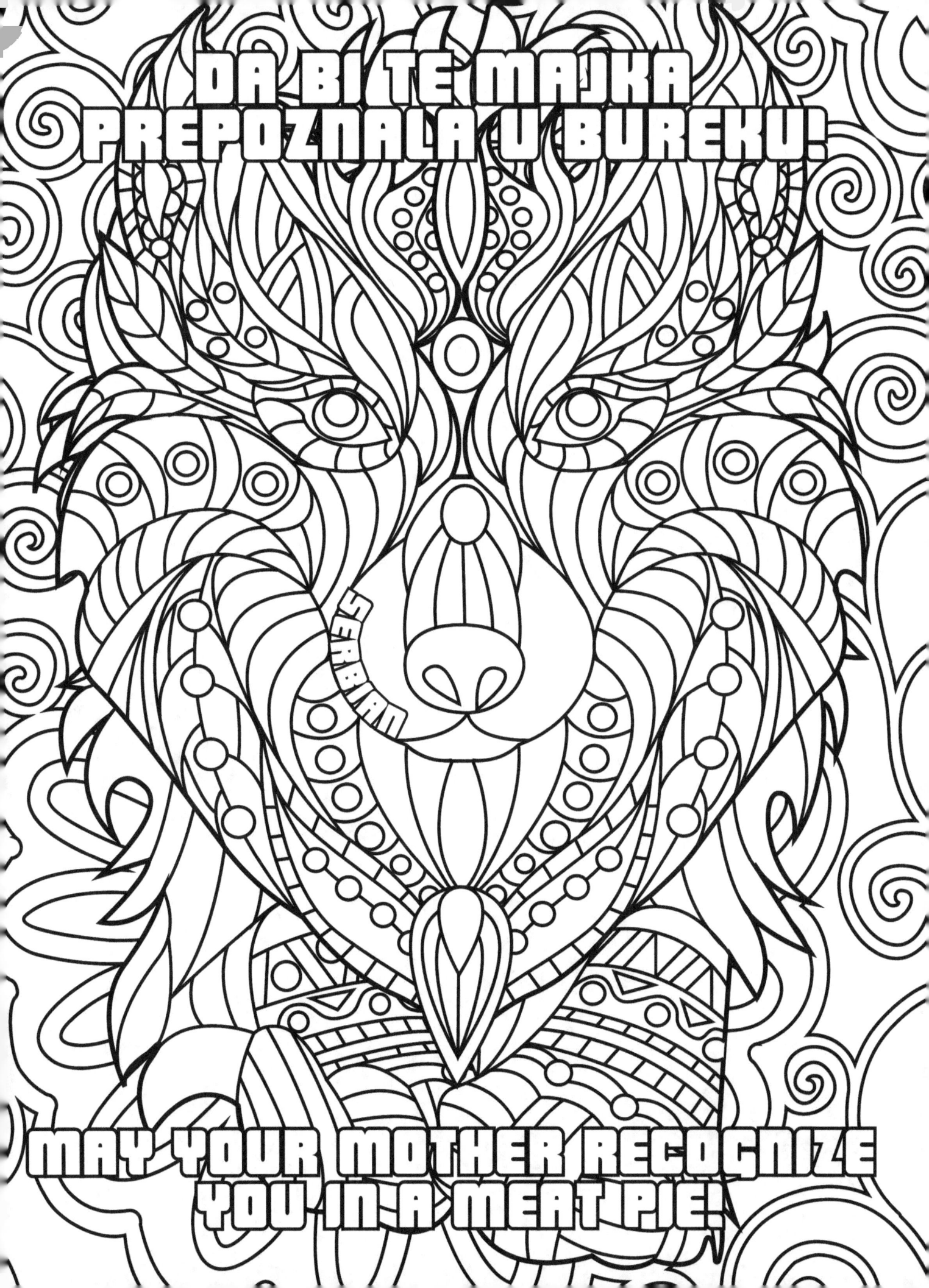

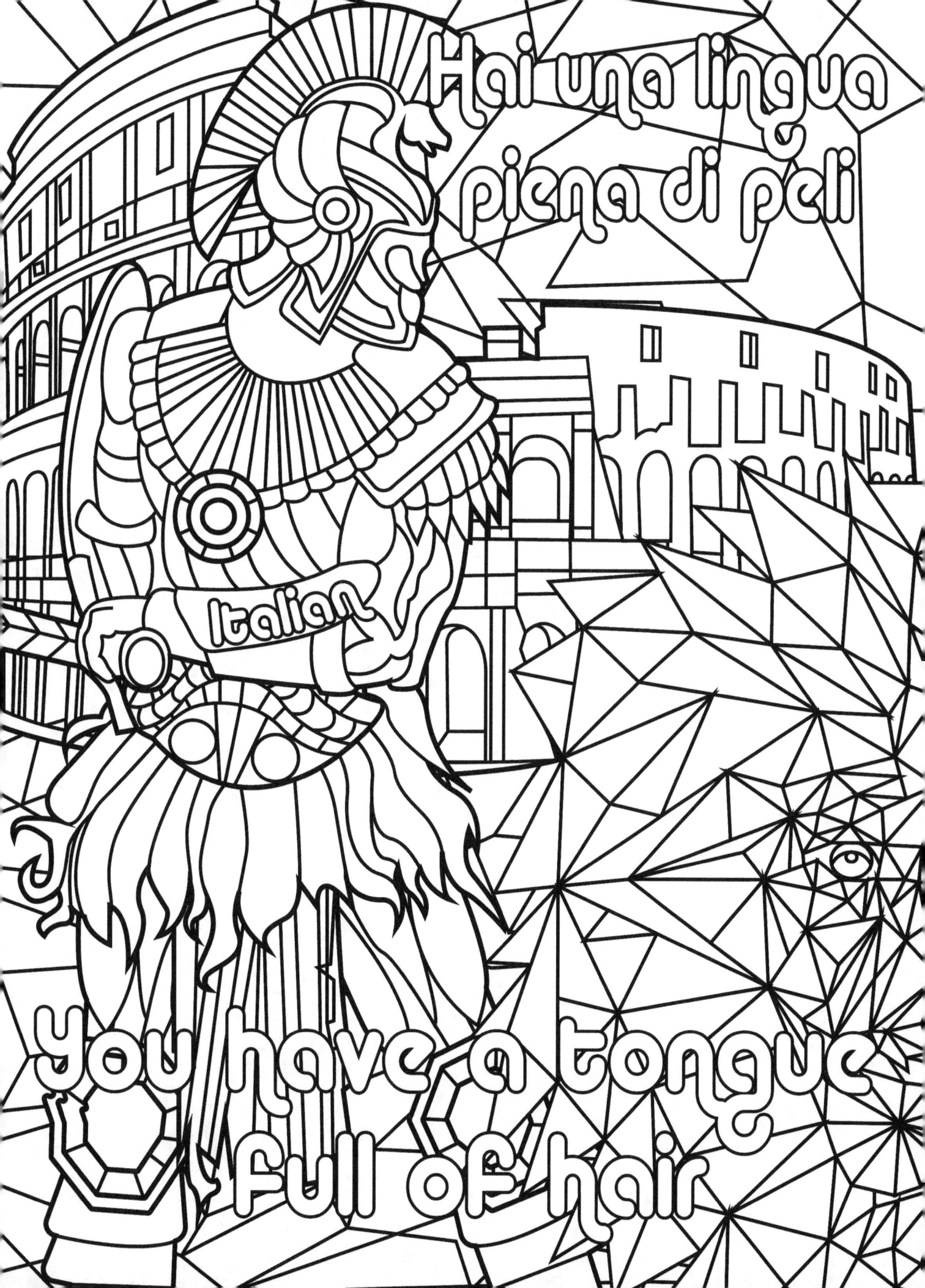

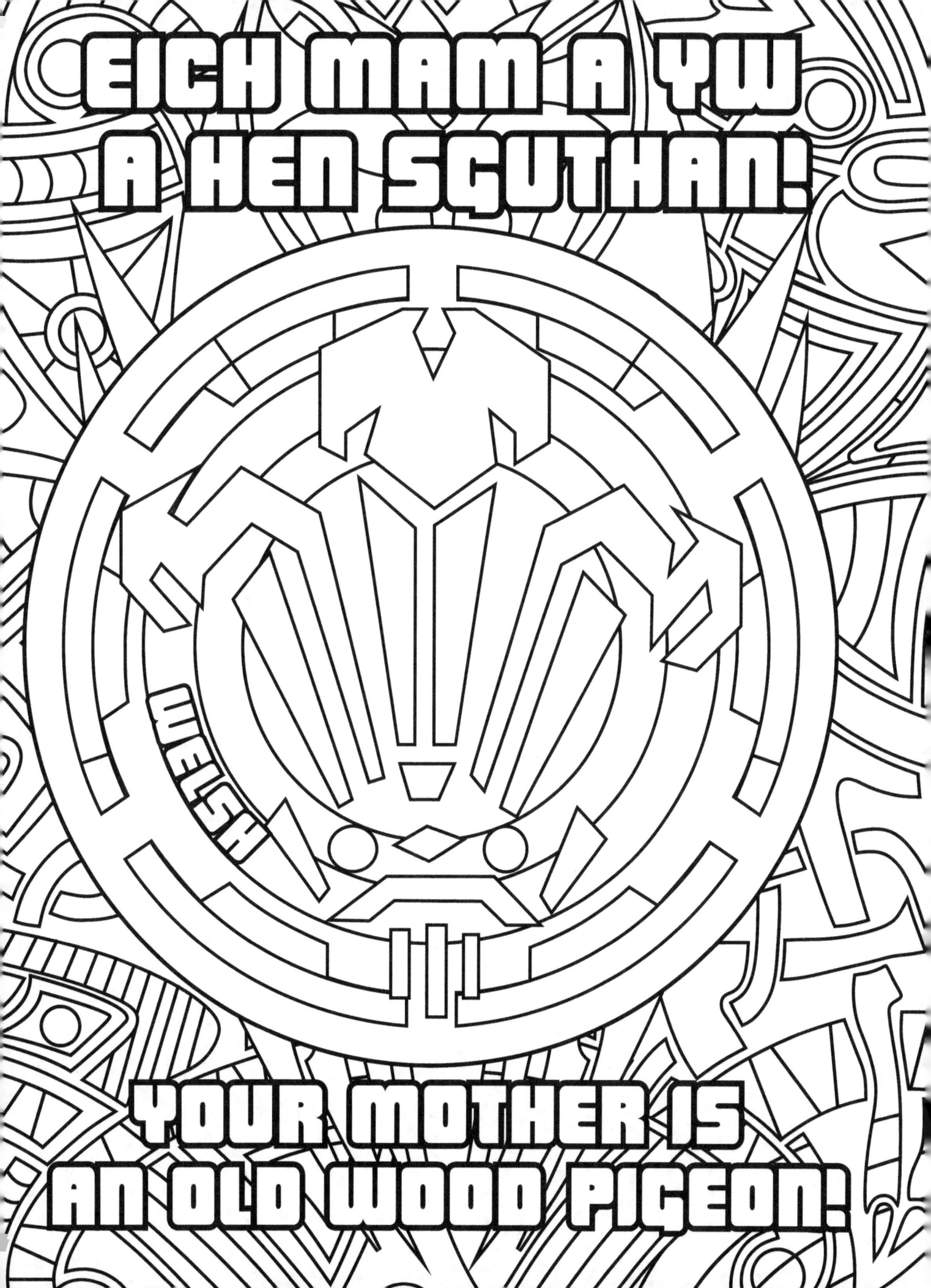

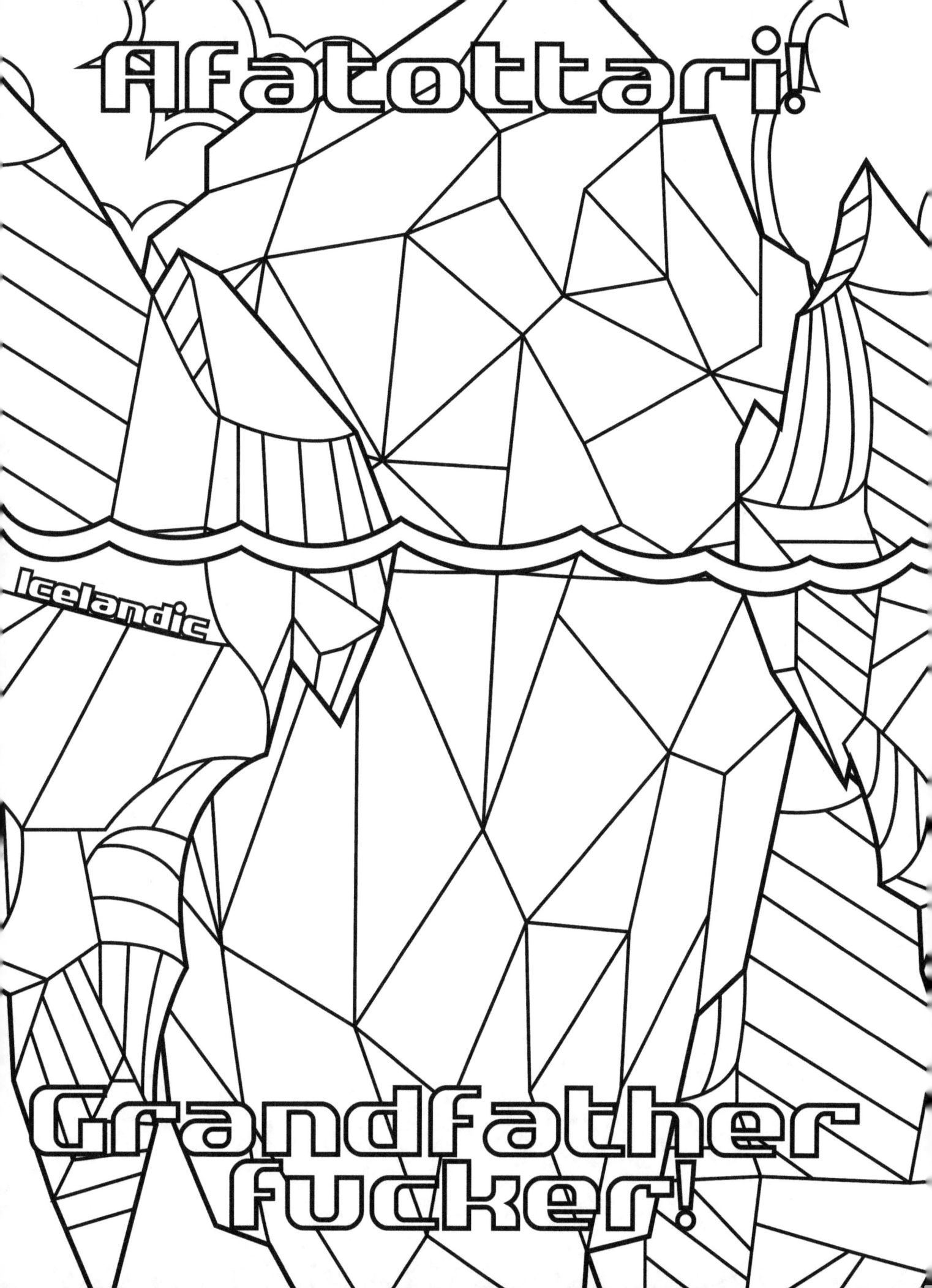

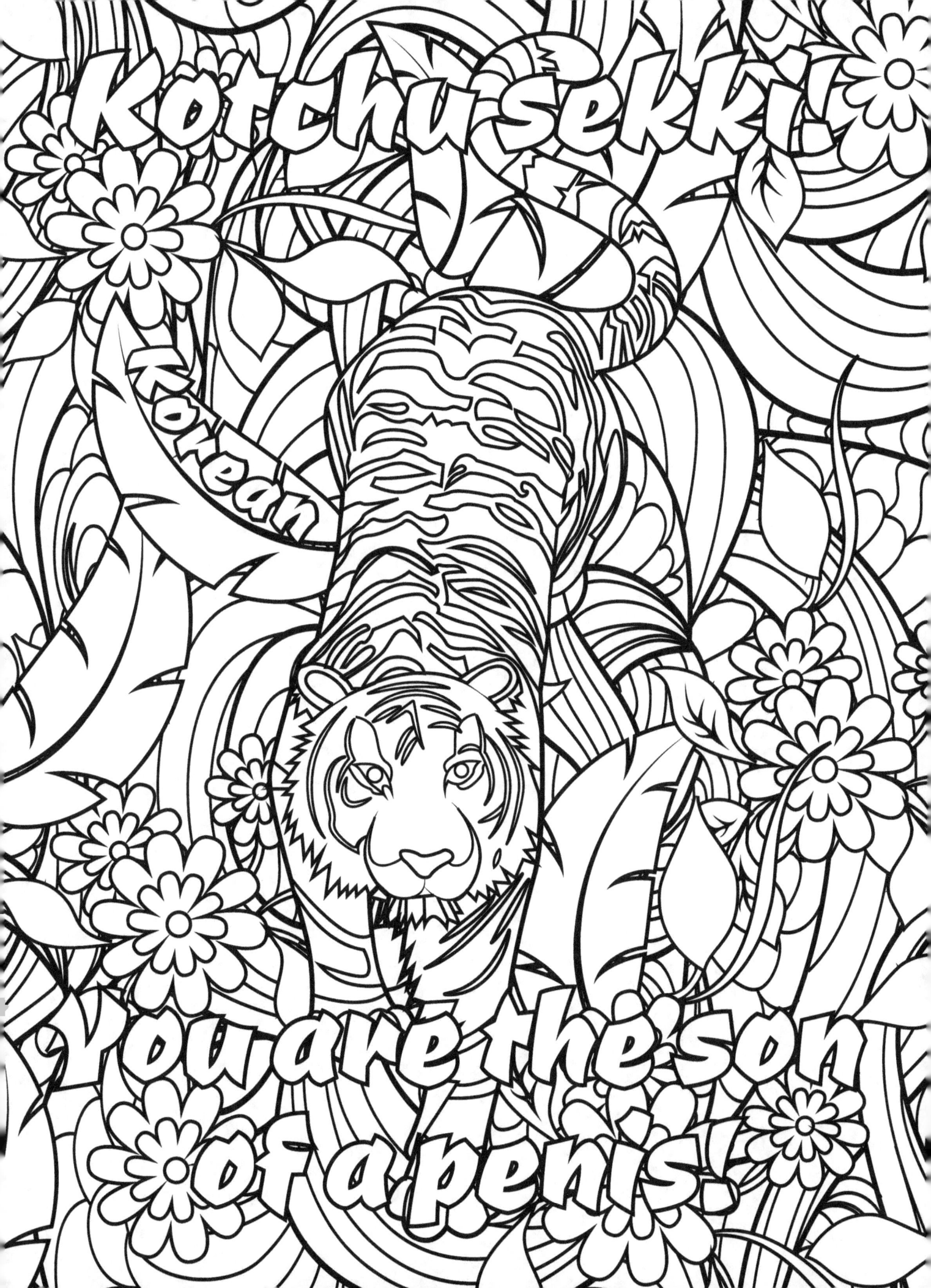

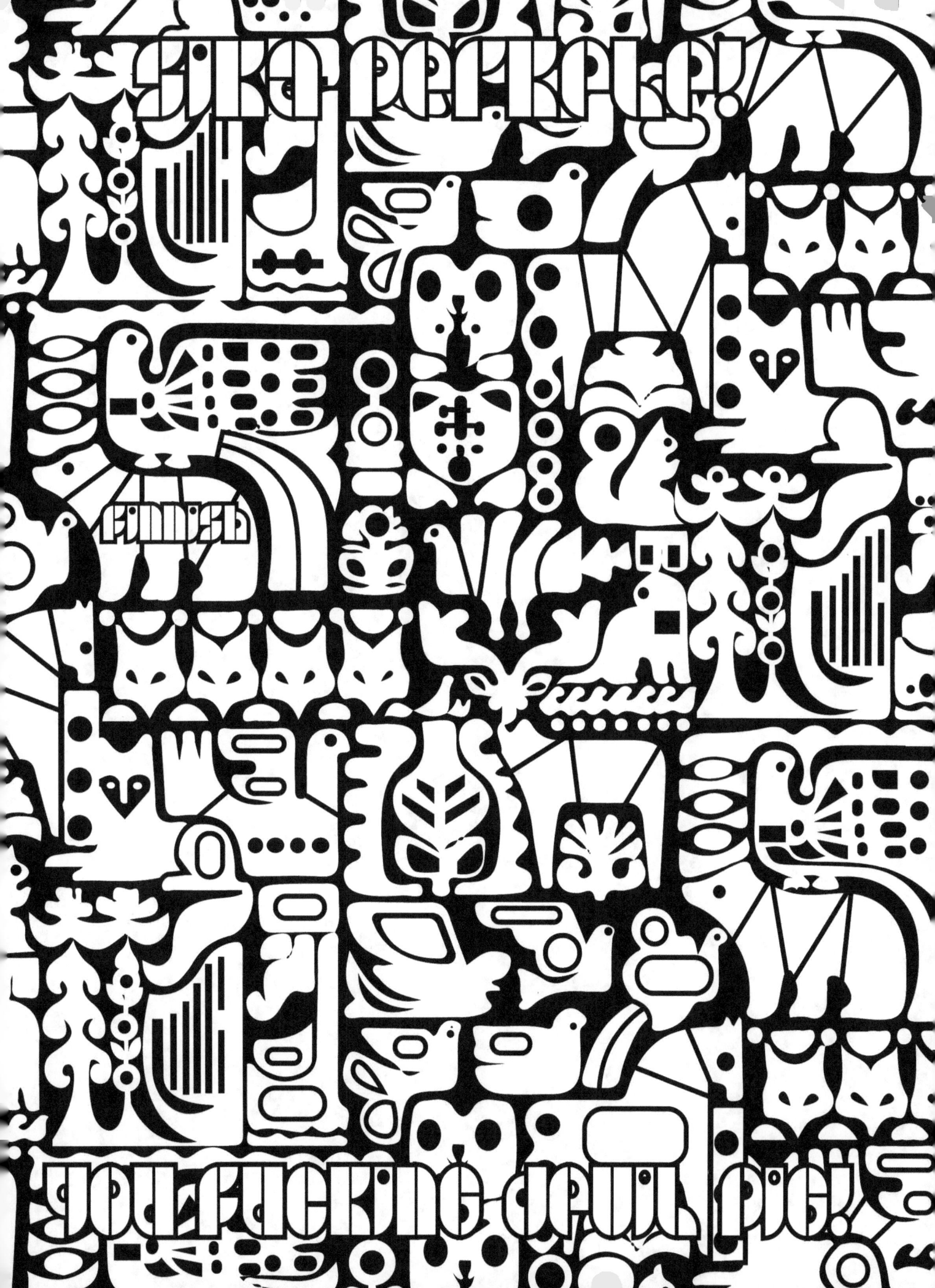

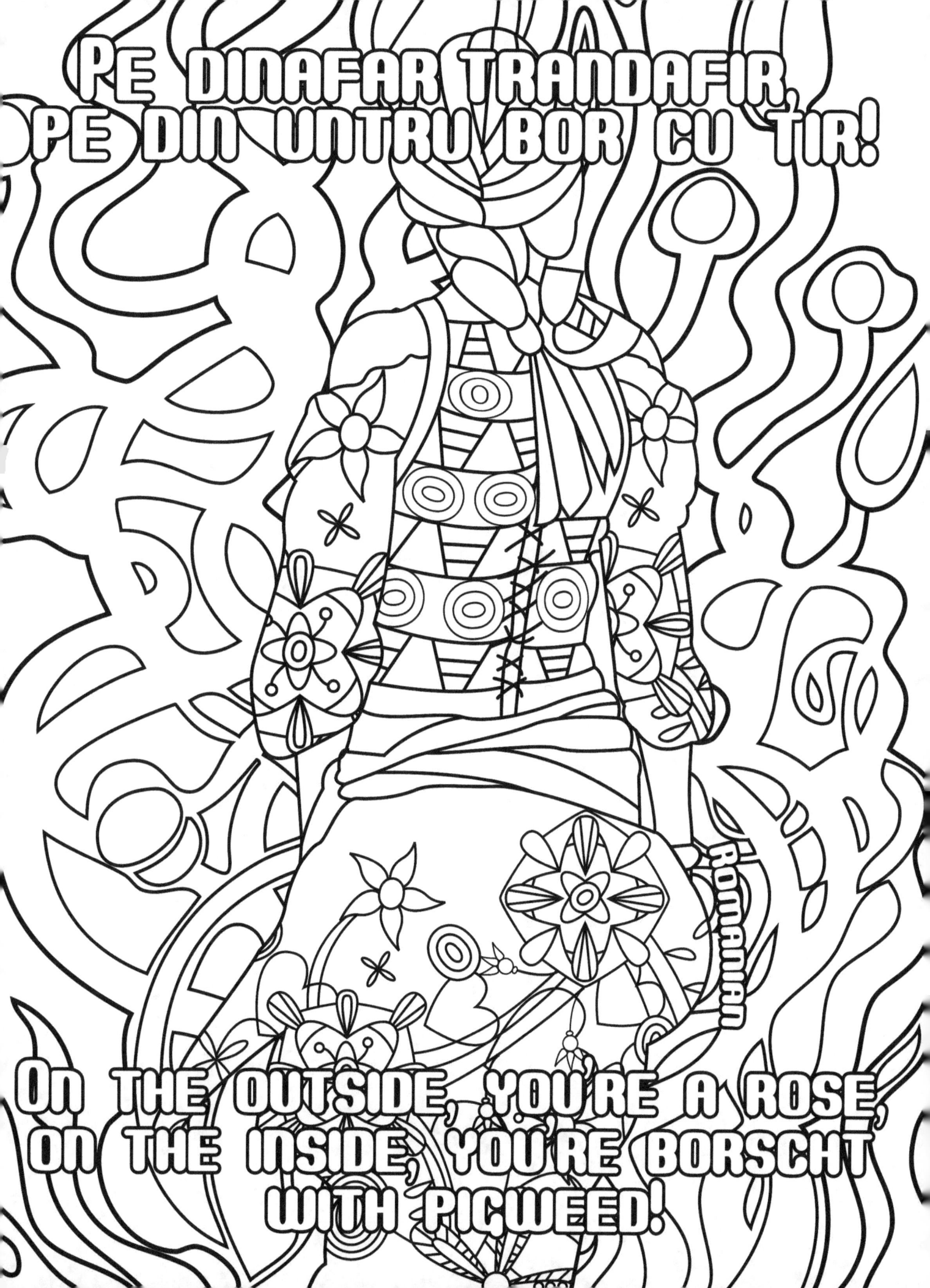

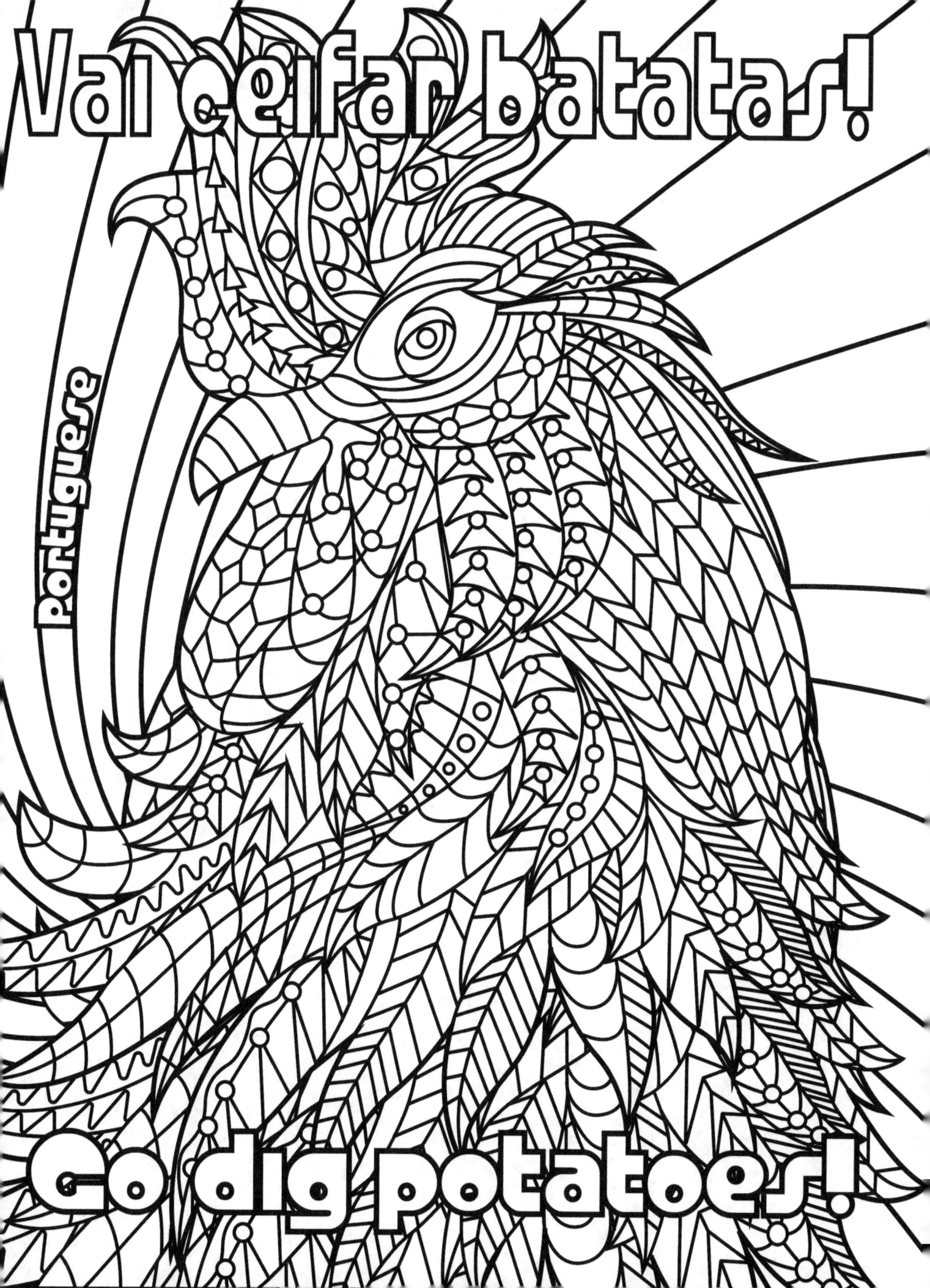

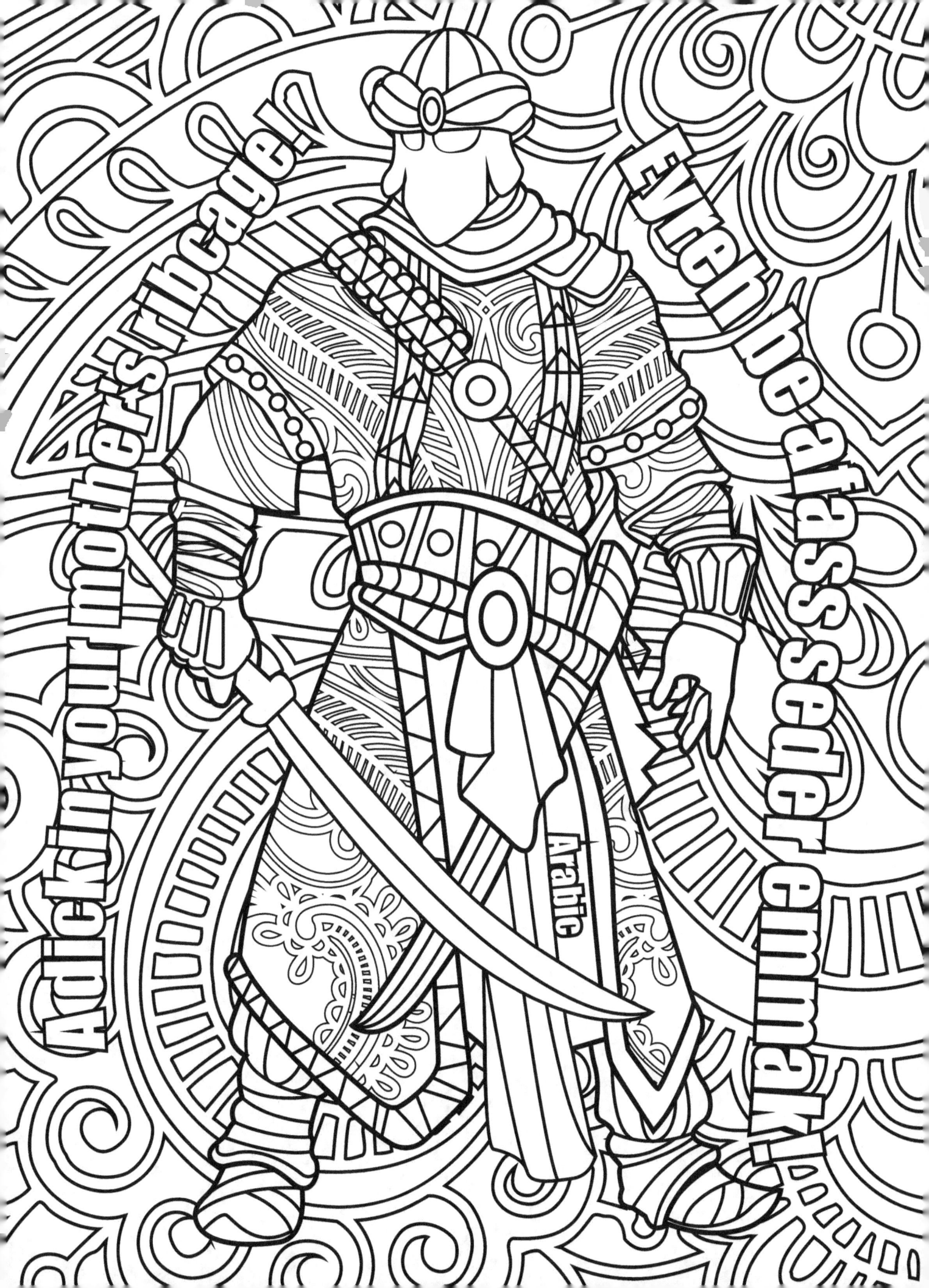

A dick in your mother's ribcage!

Evreninafassseder emmak

Arabic

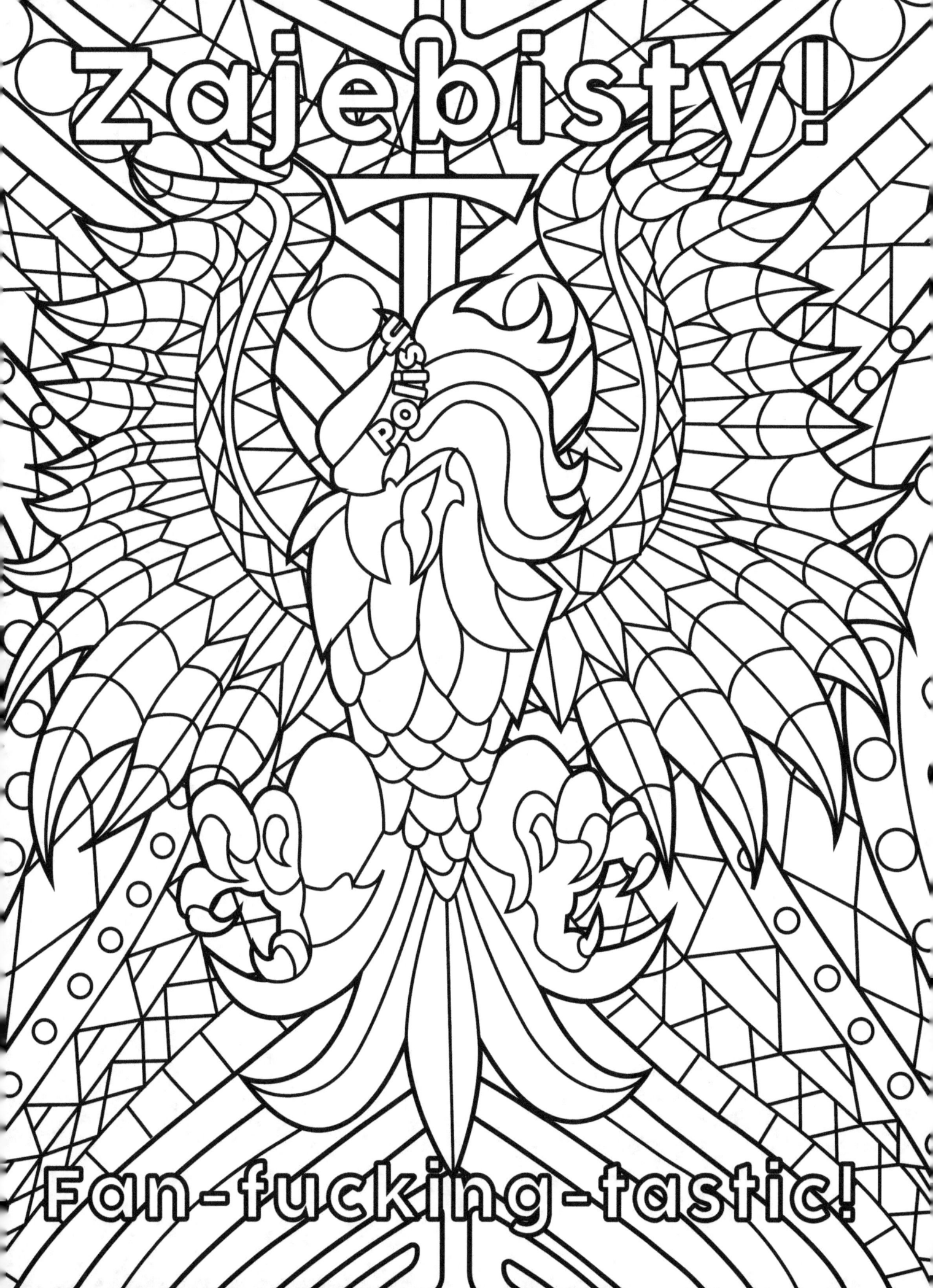

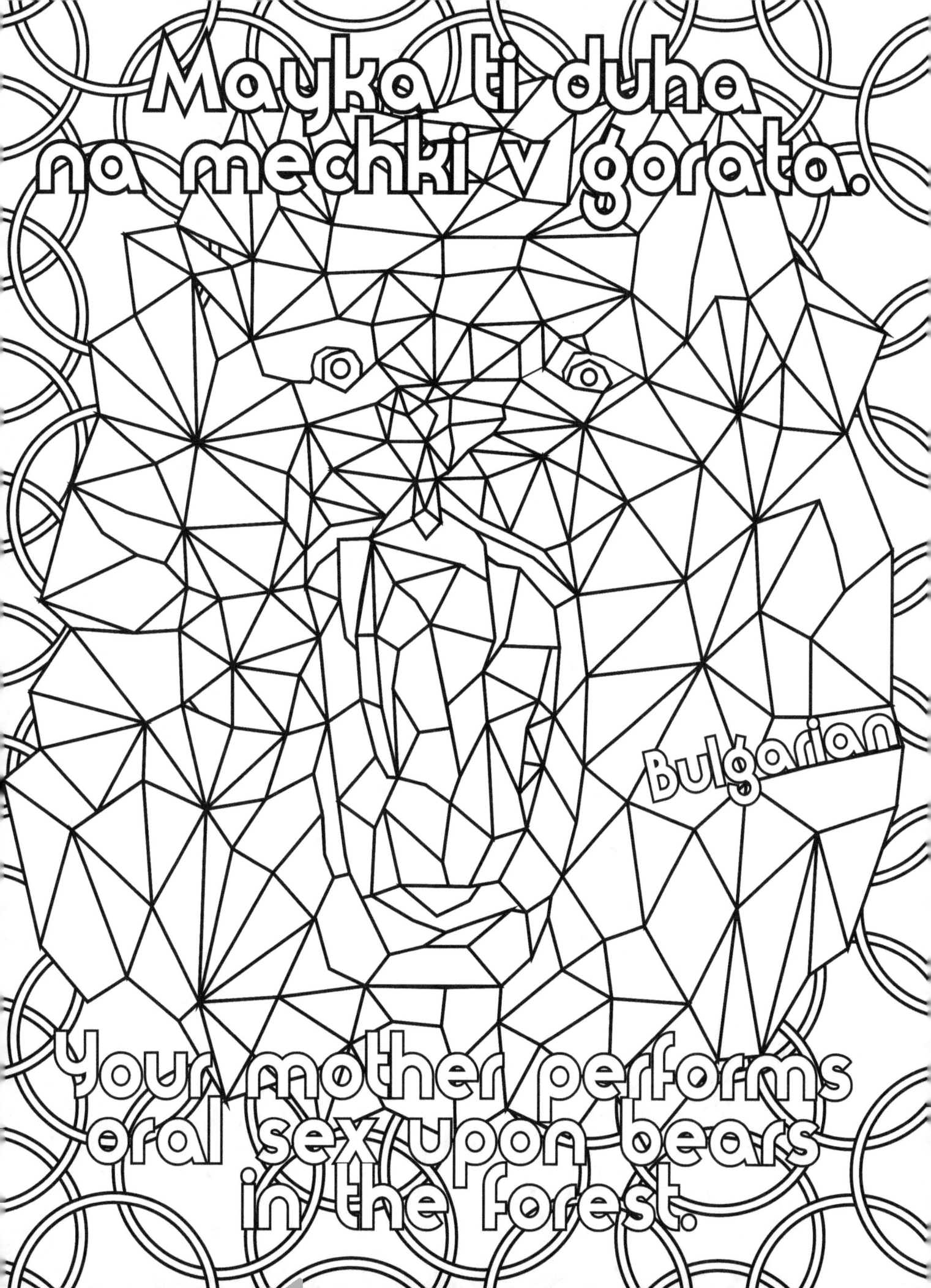

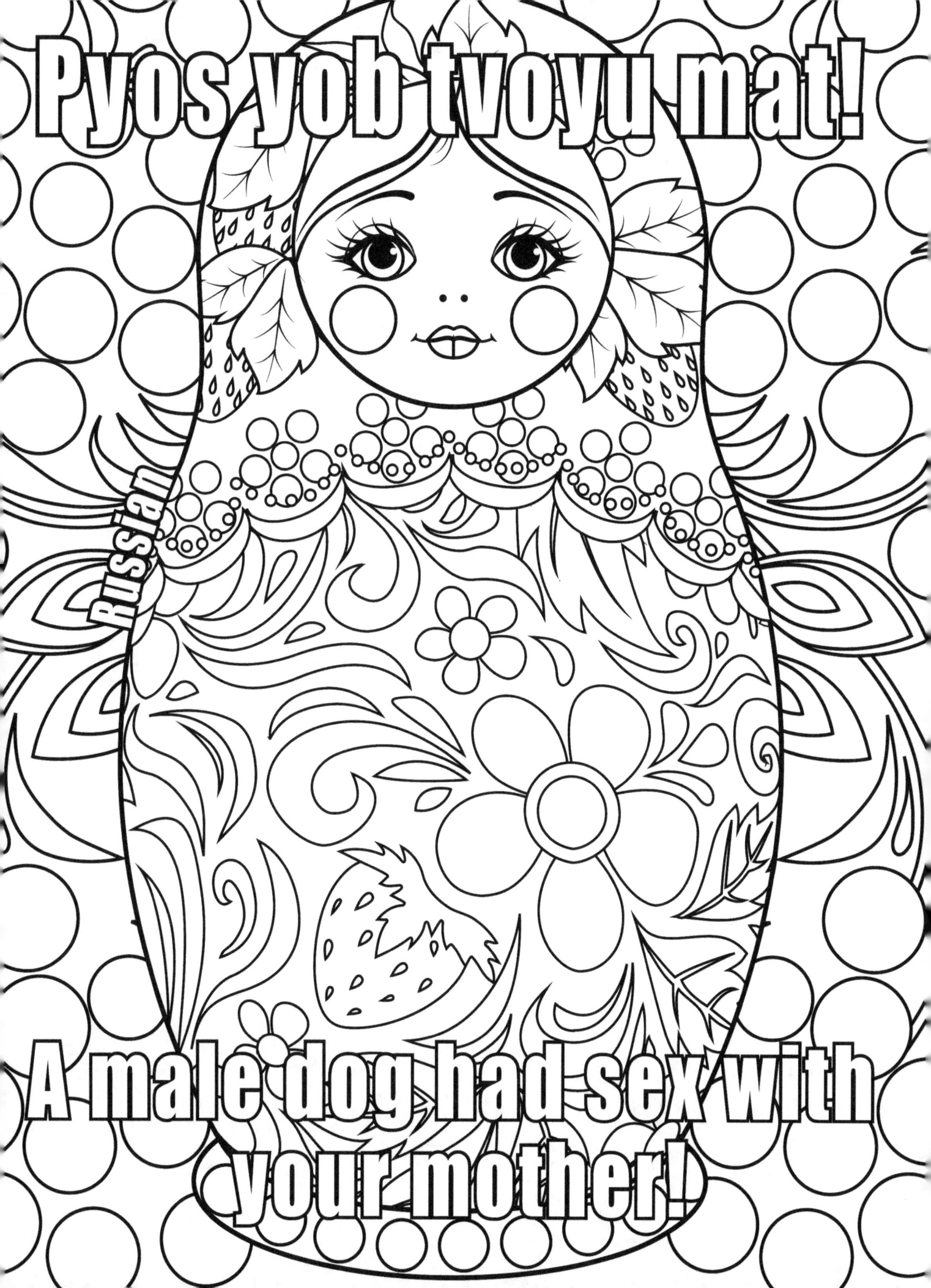

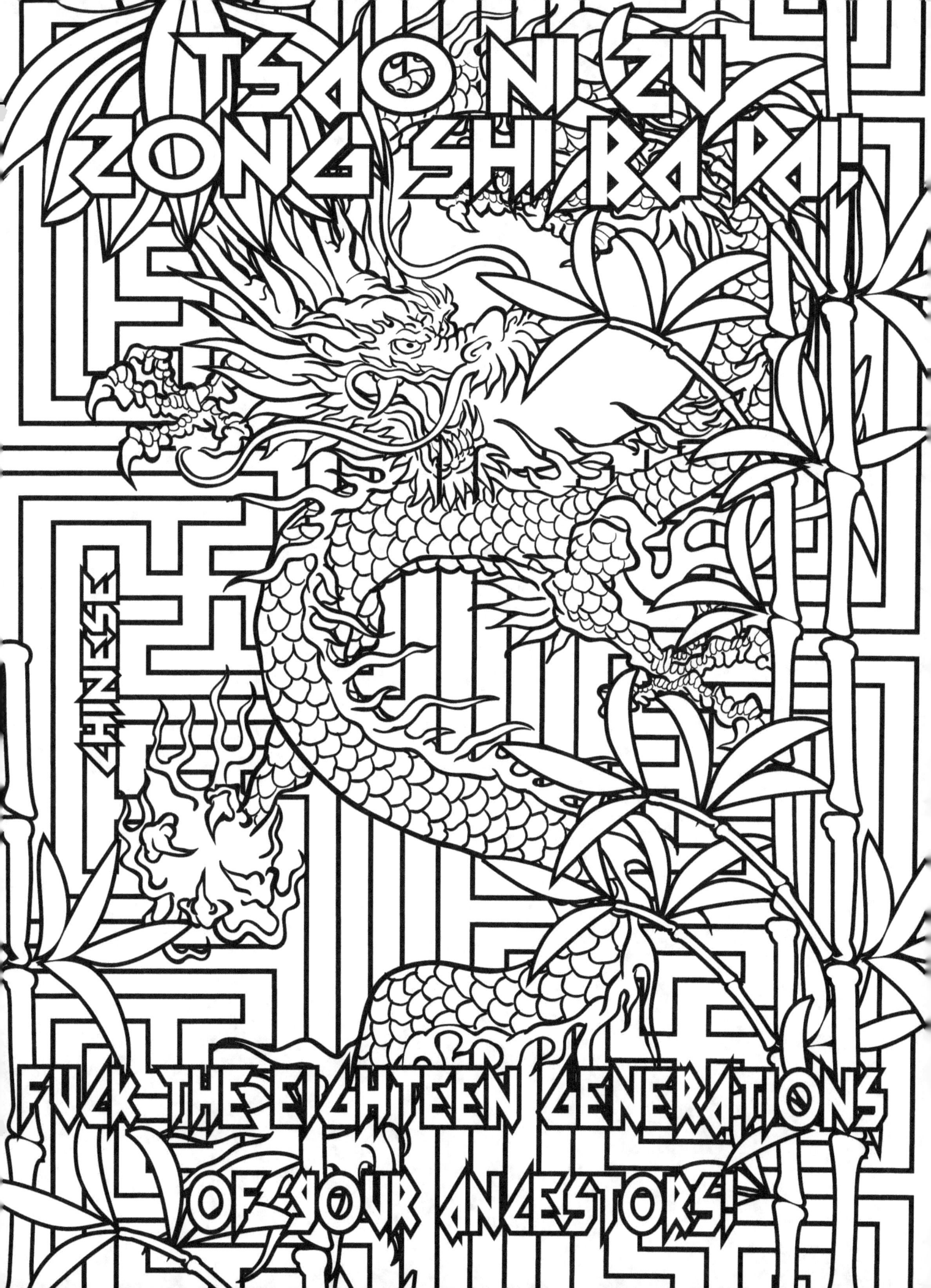

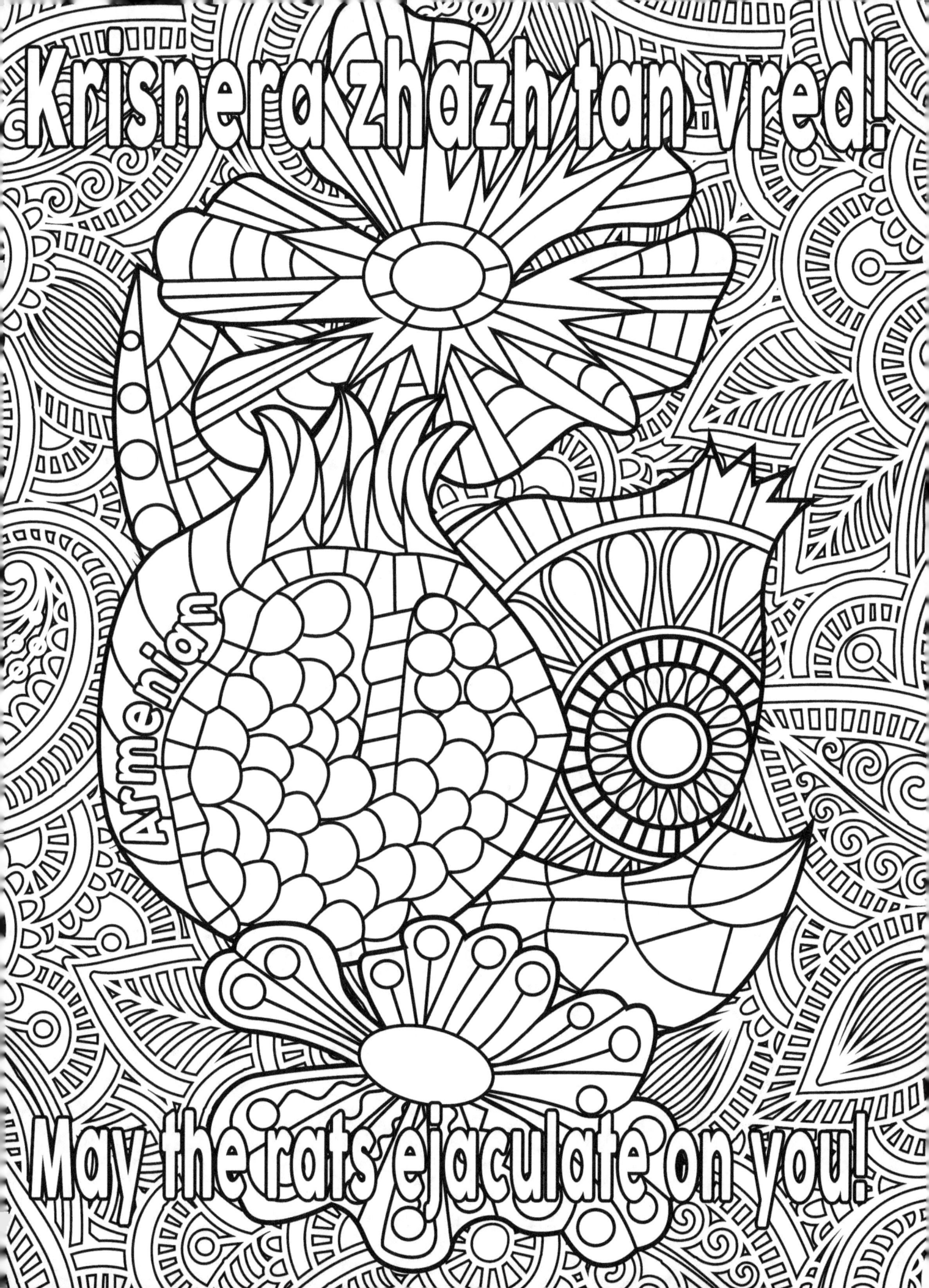

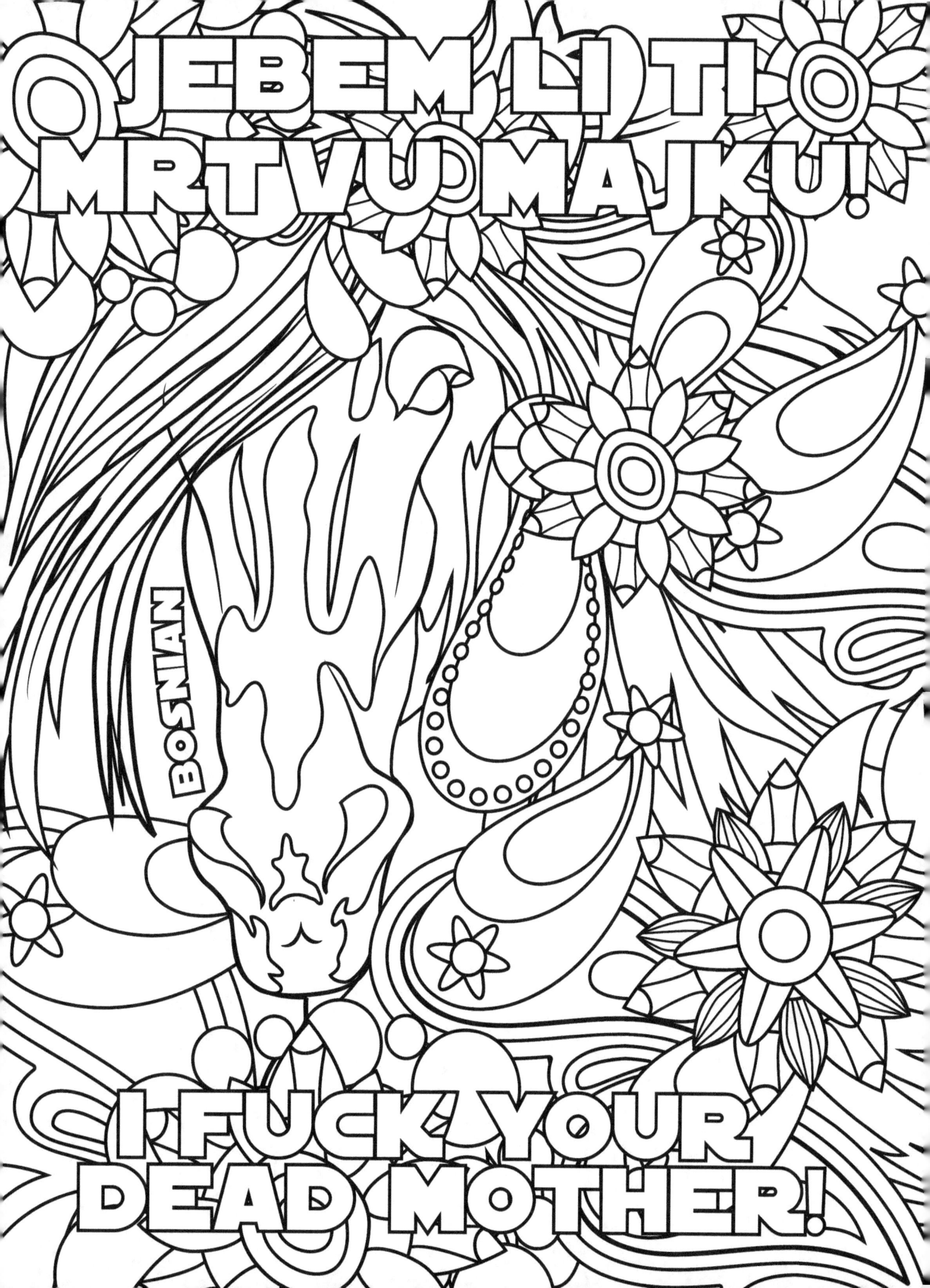

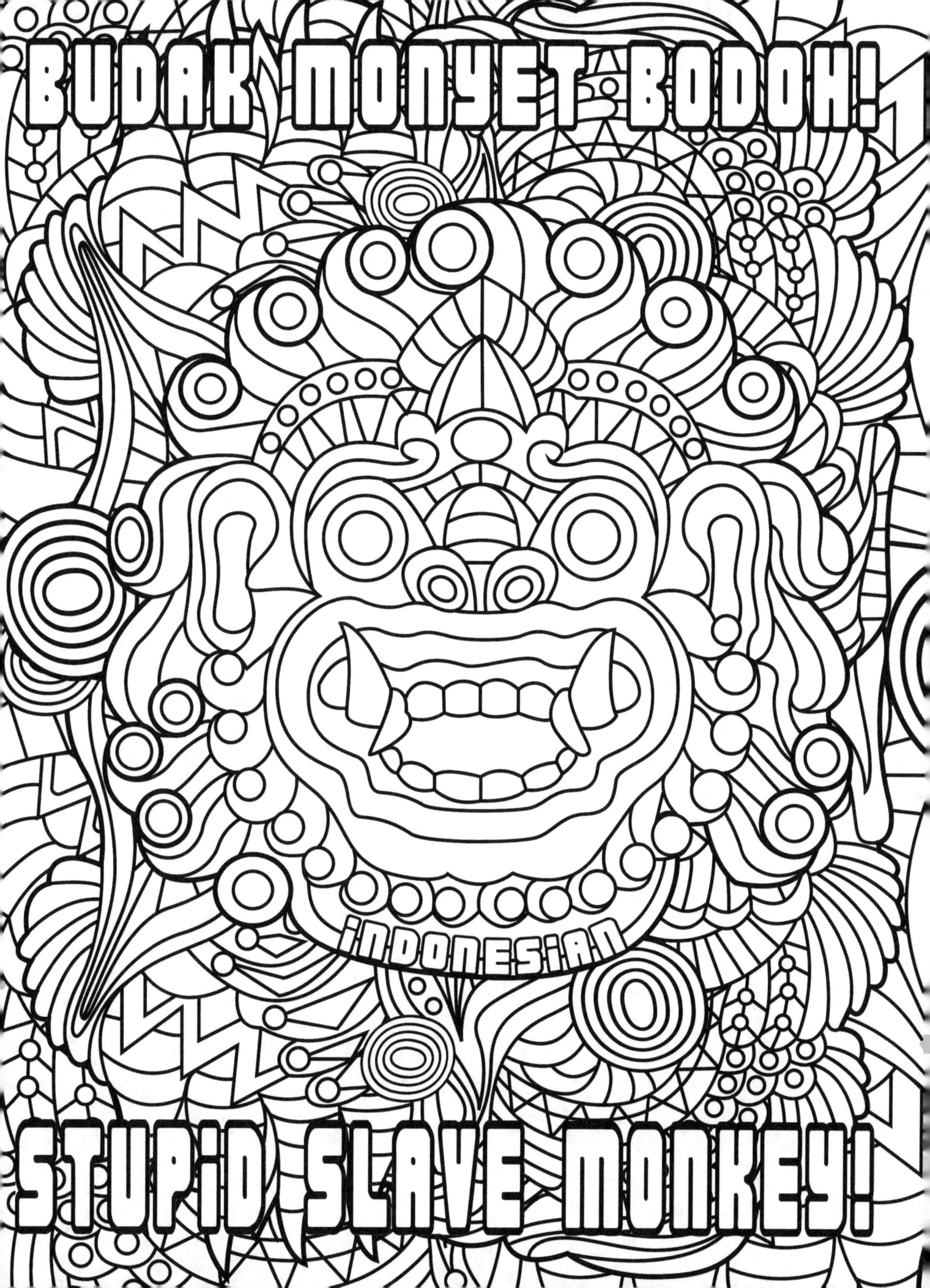

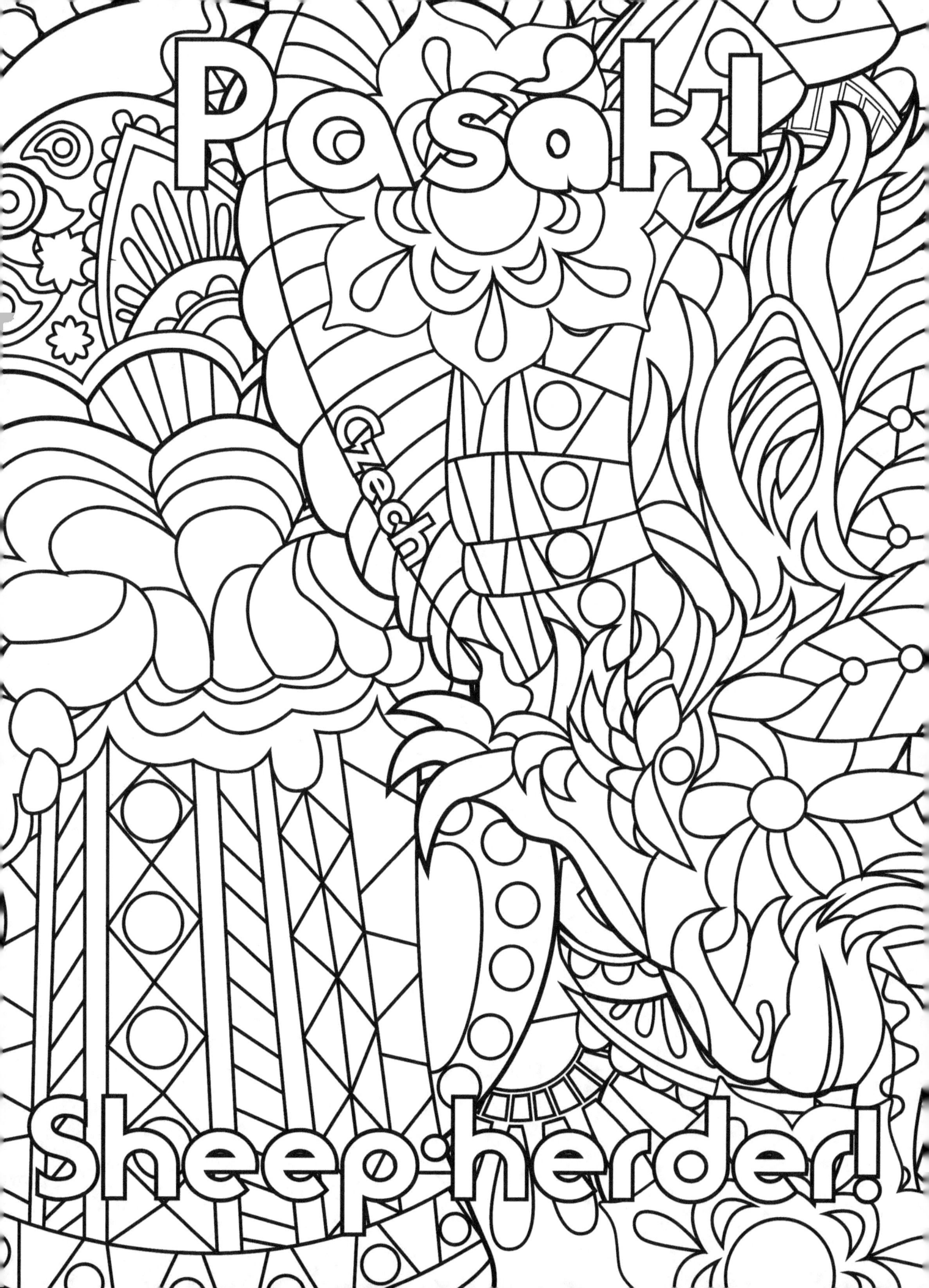

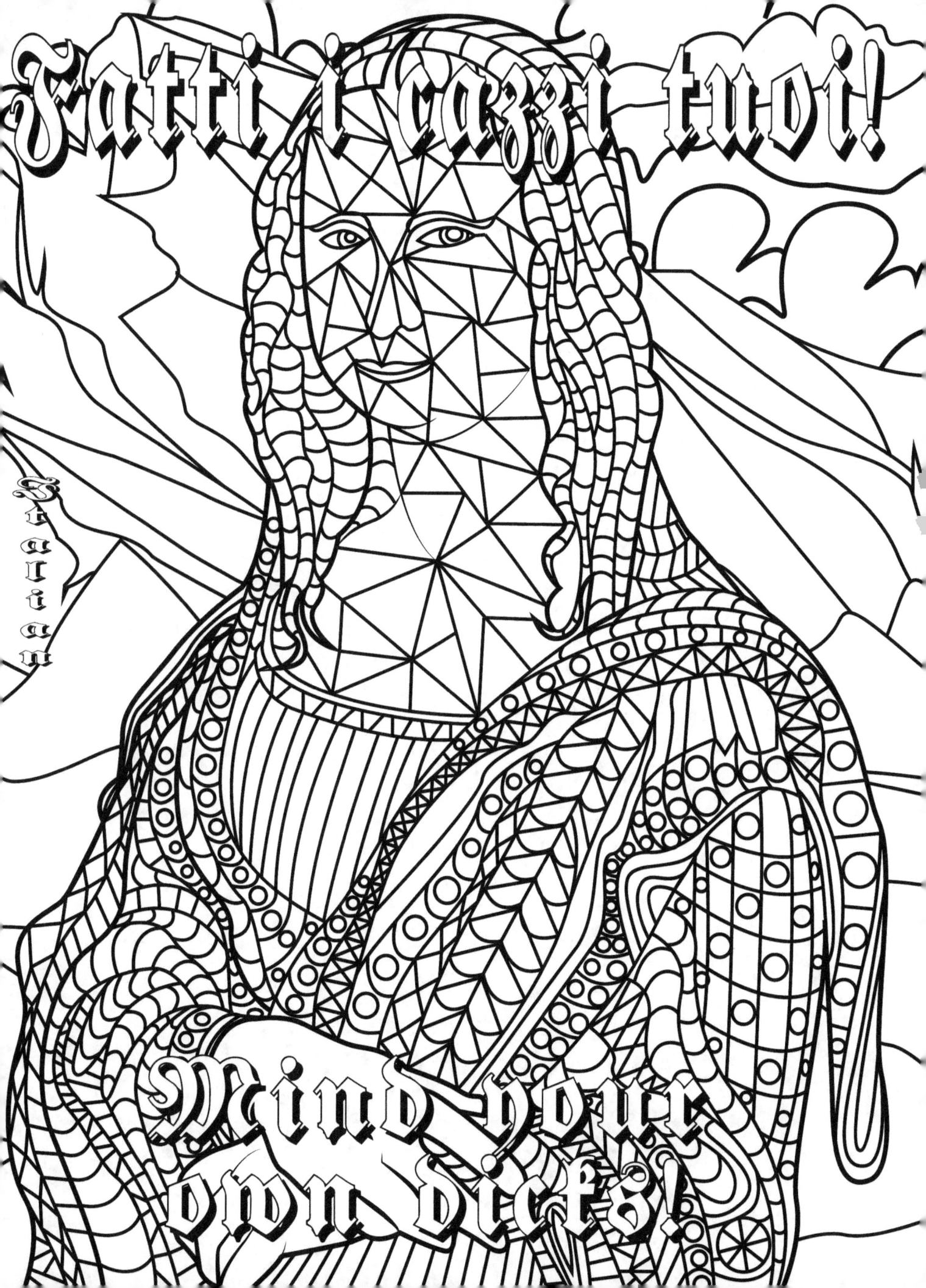

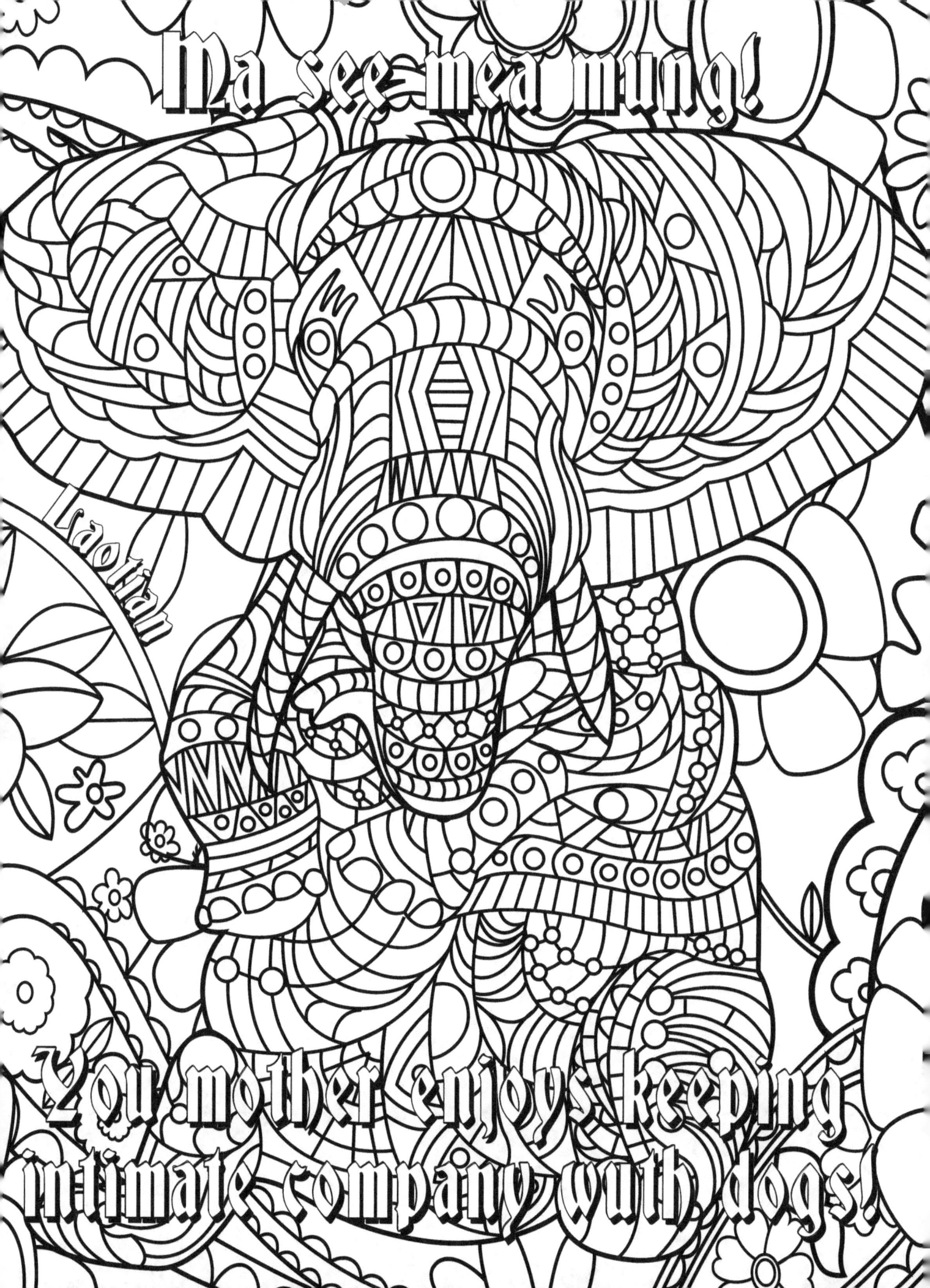

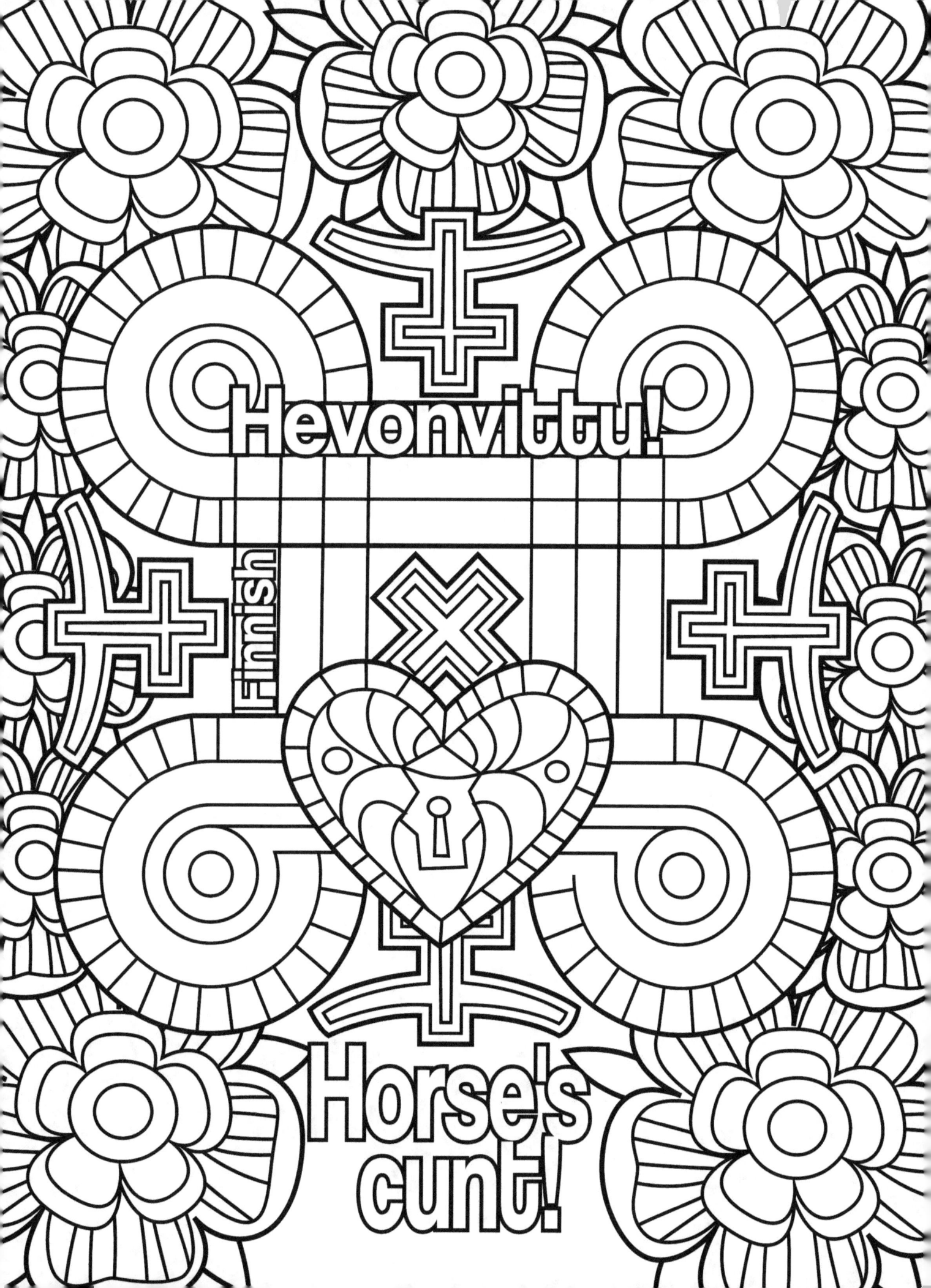

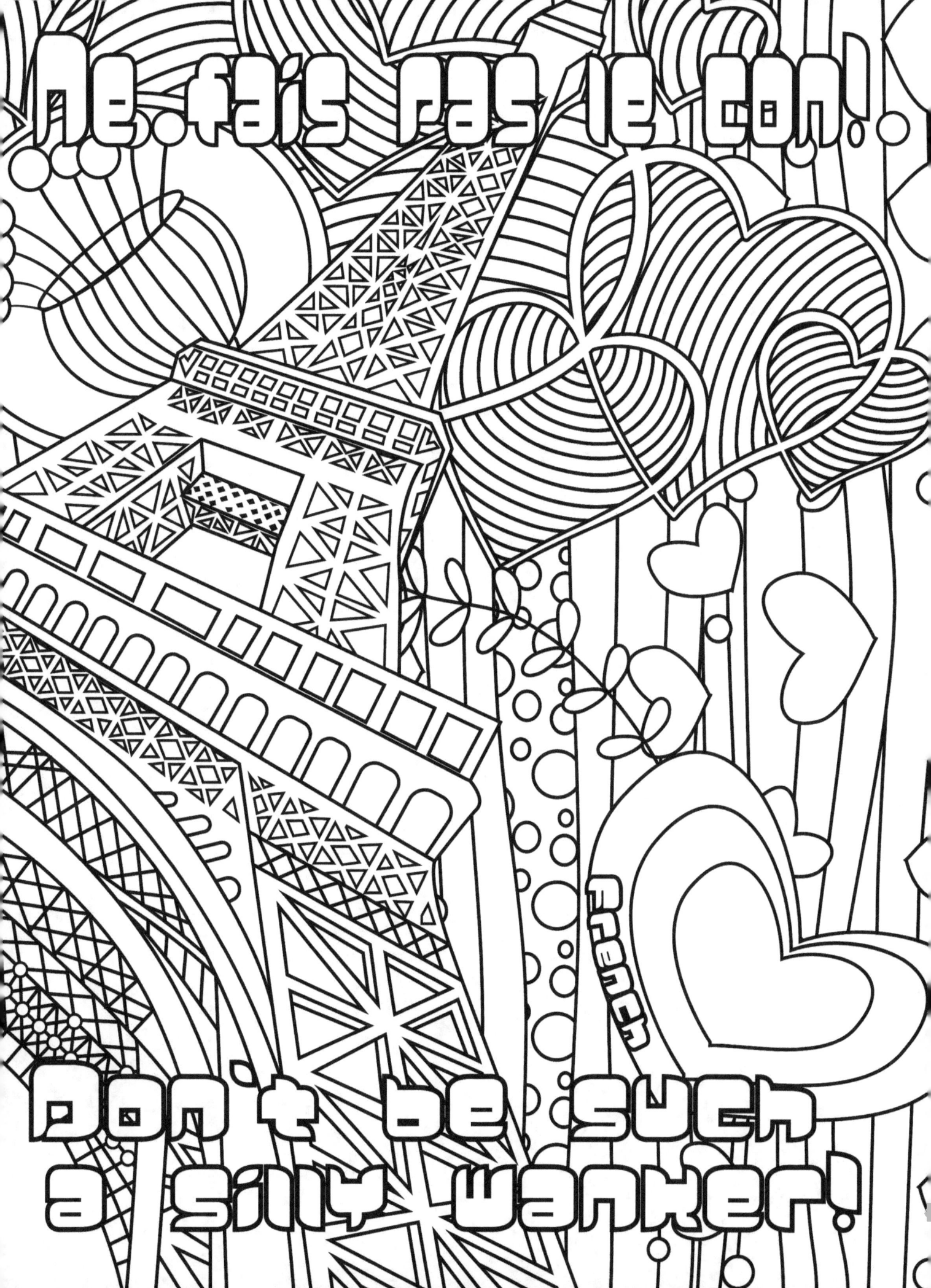

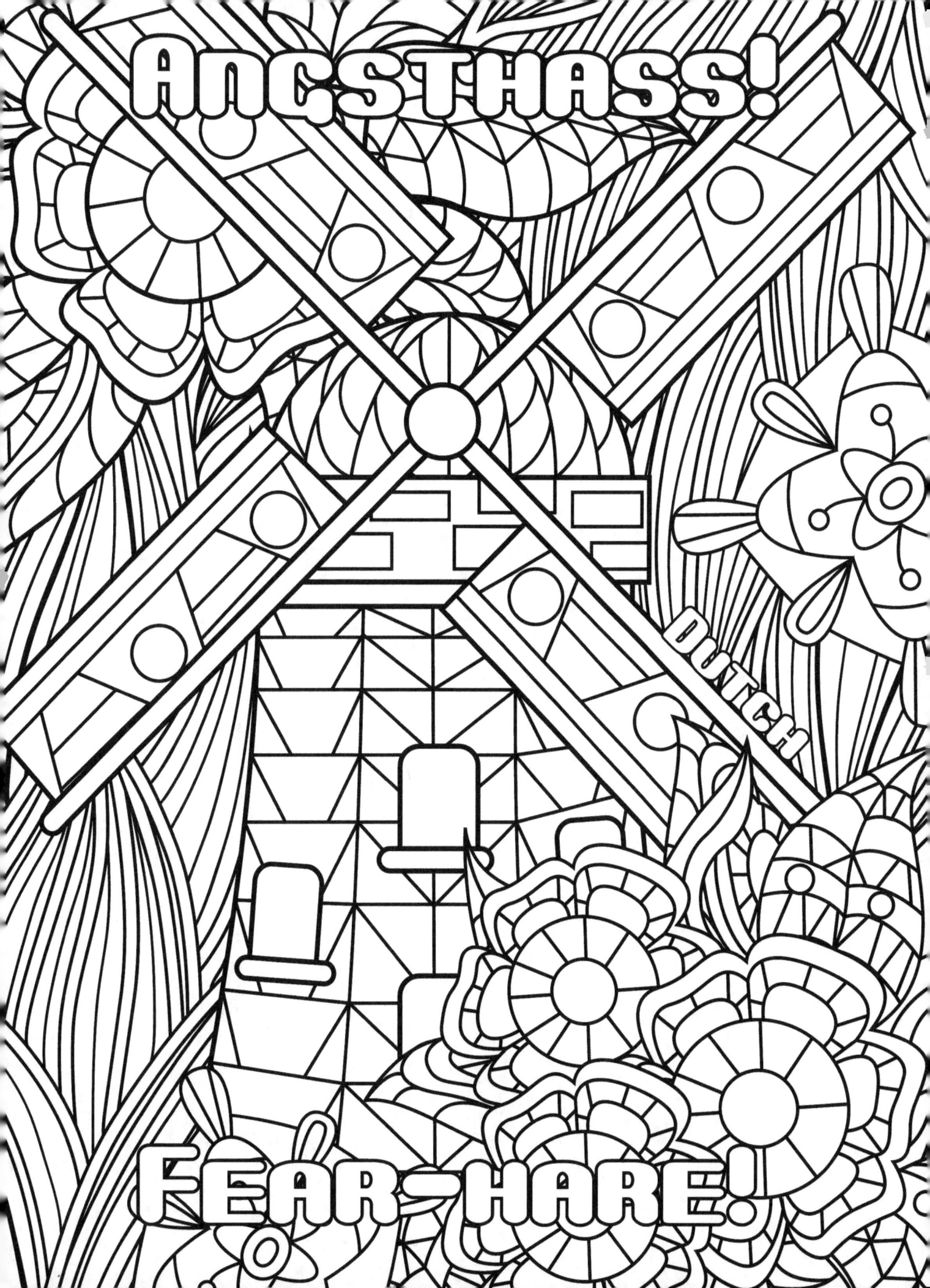

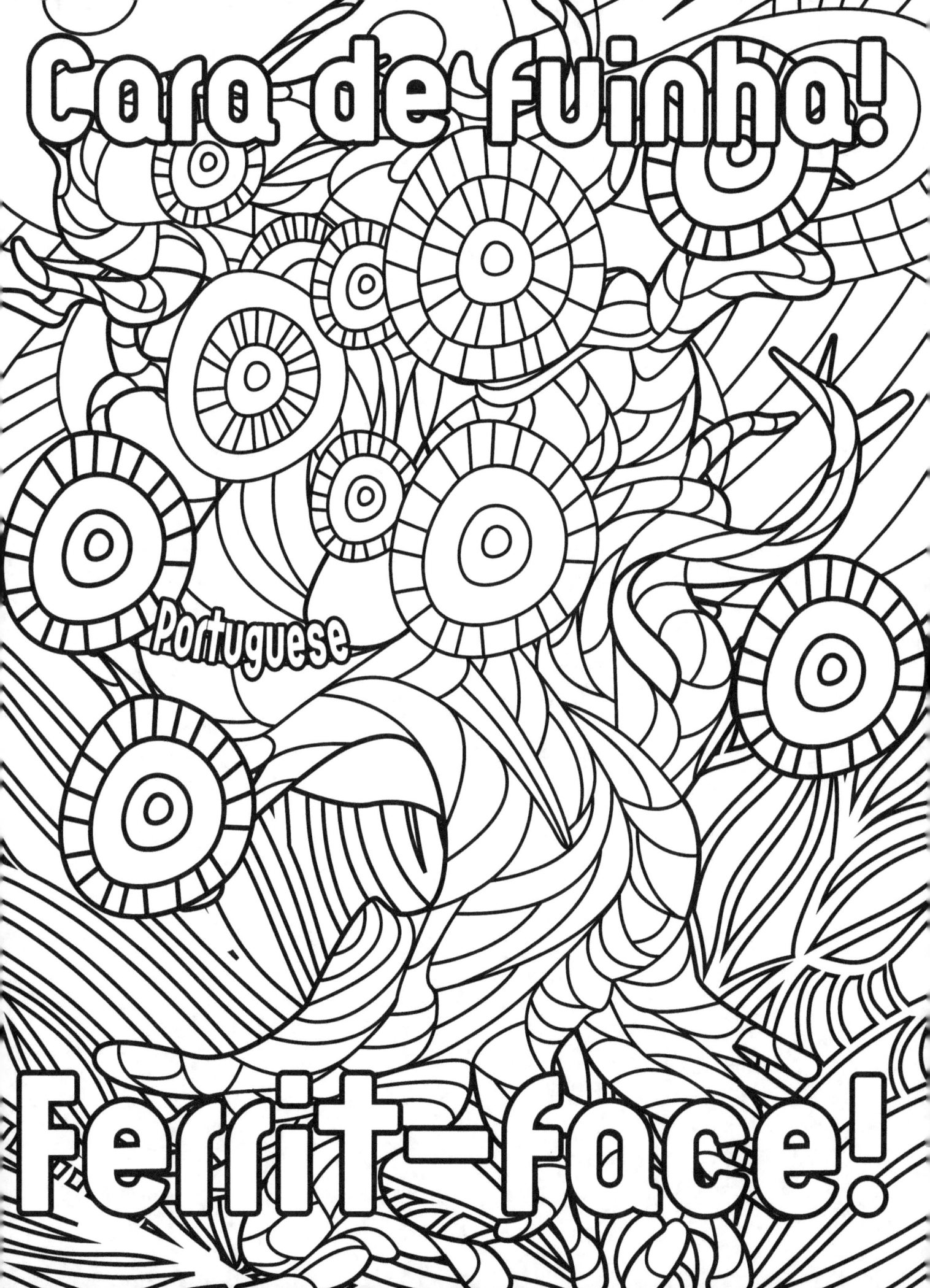

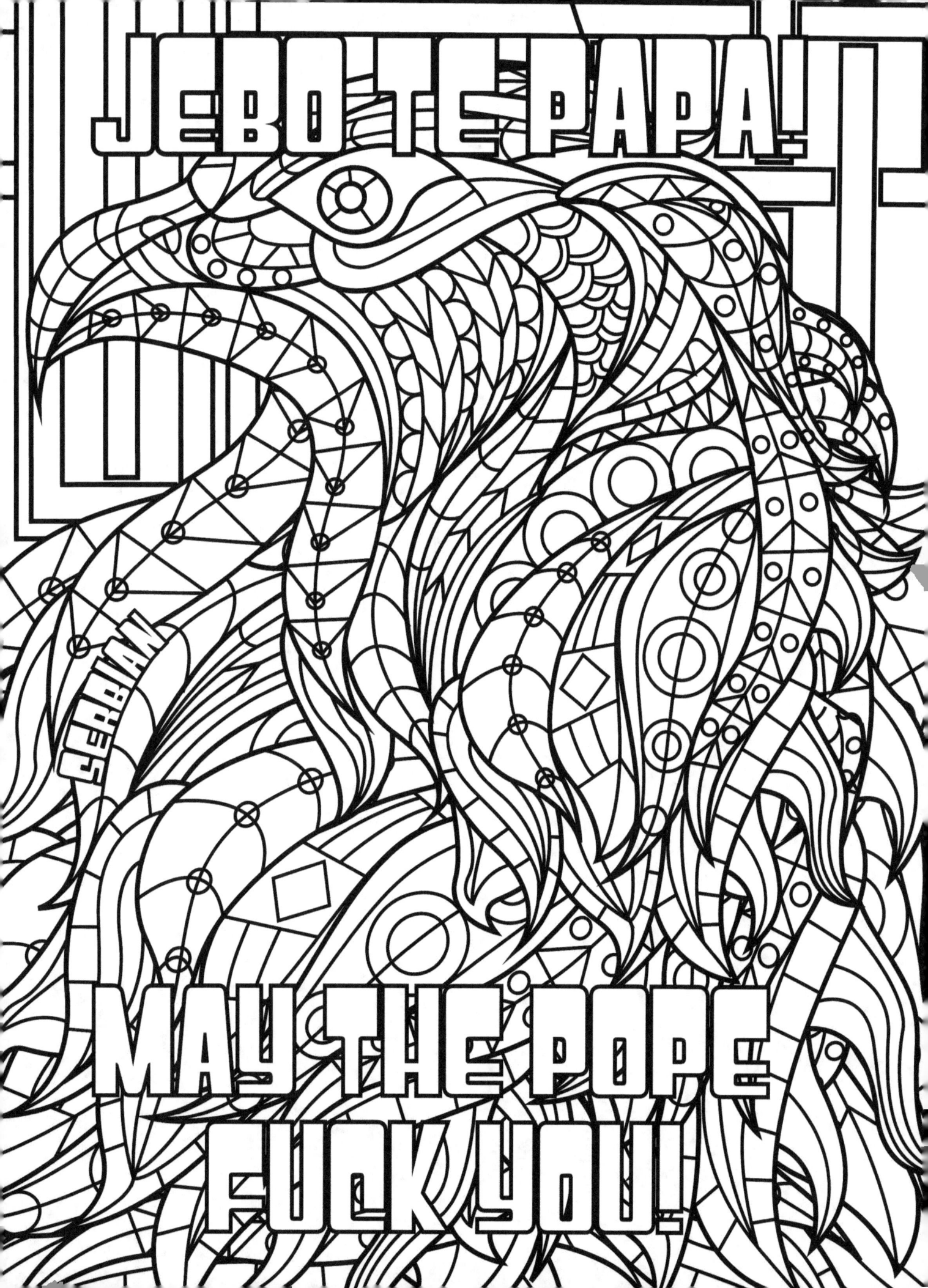

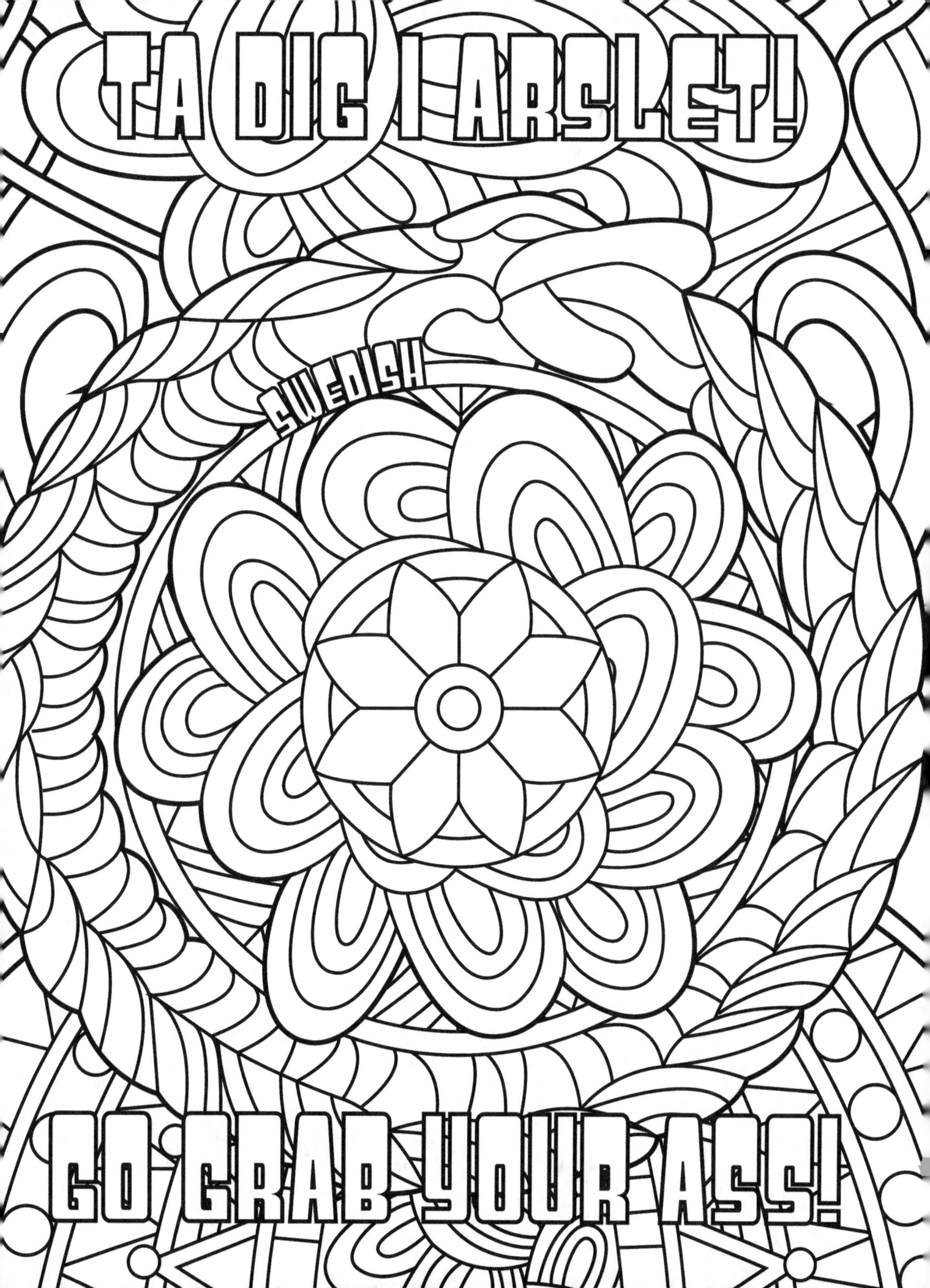

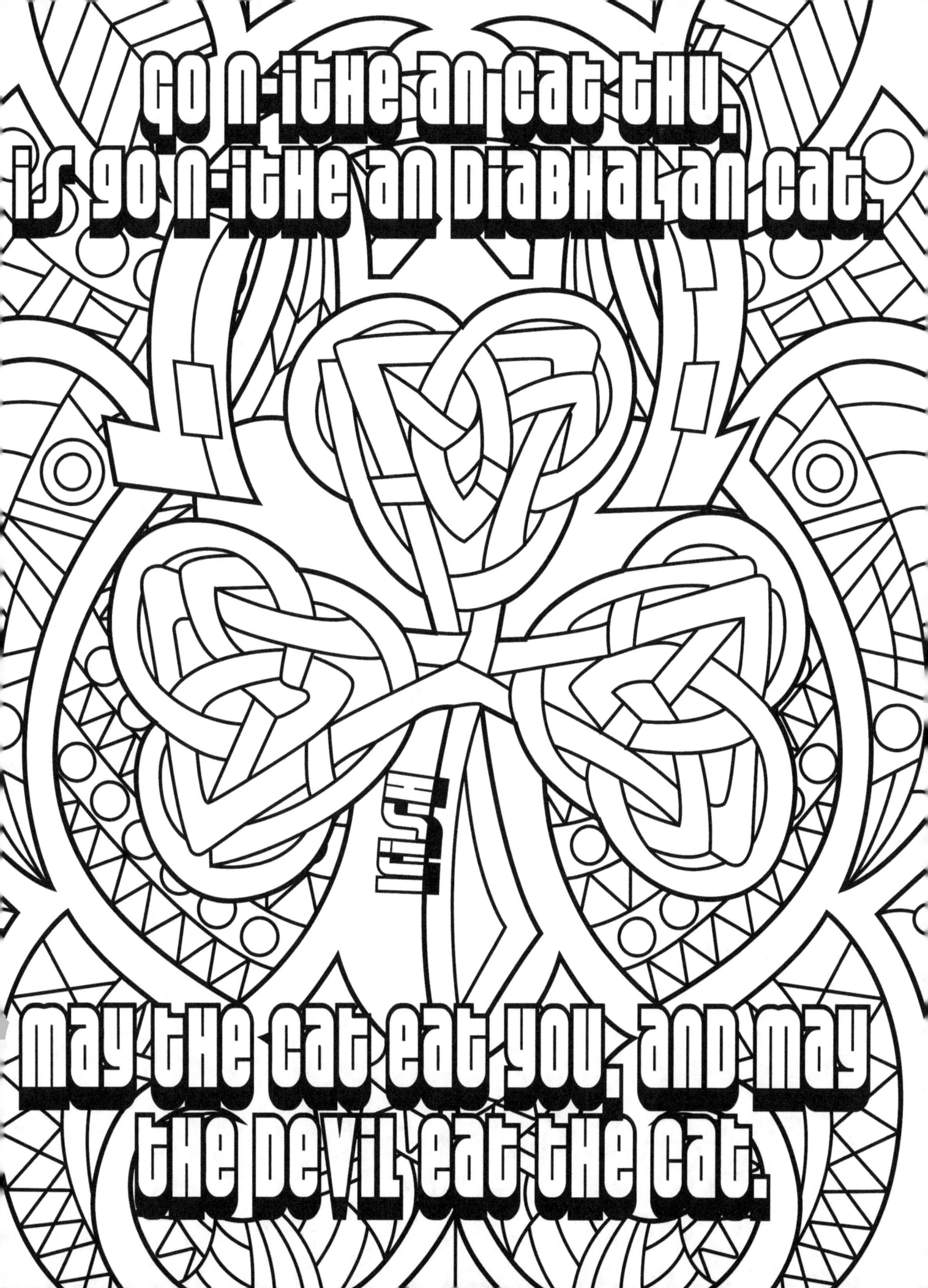

Go n-ithe an cat thú, is go n-ithe an diabhal an cat.

Irish

May the cat eat you, and may the devil eat the cat.

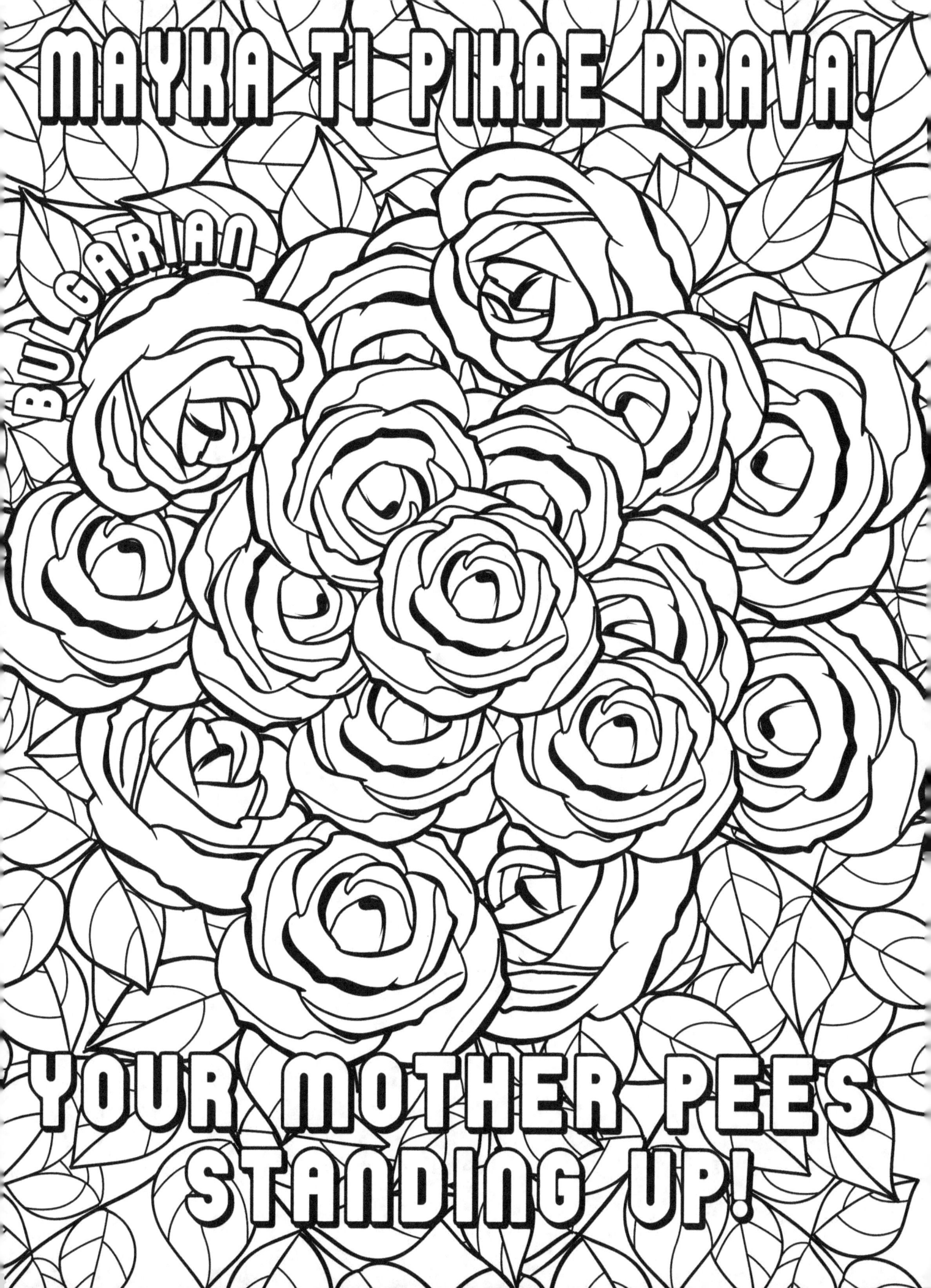

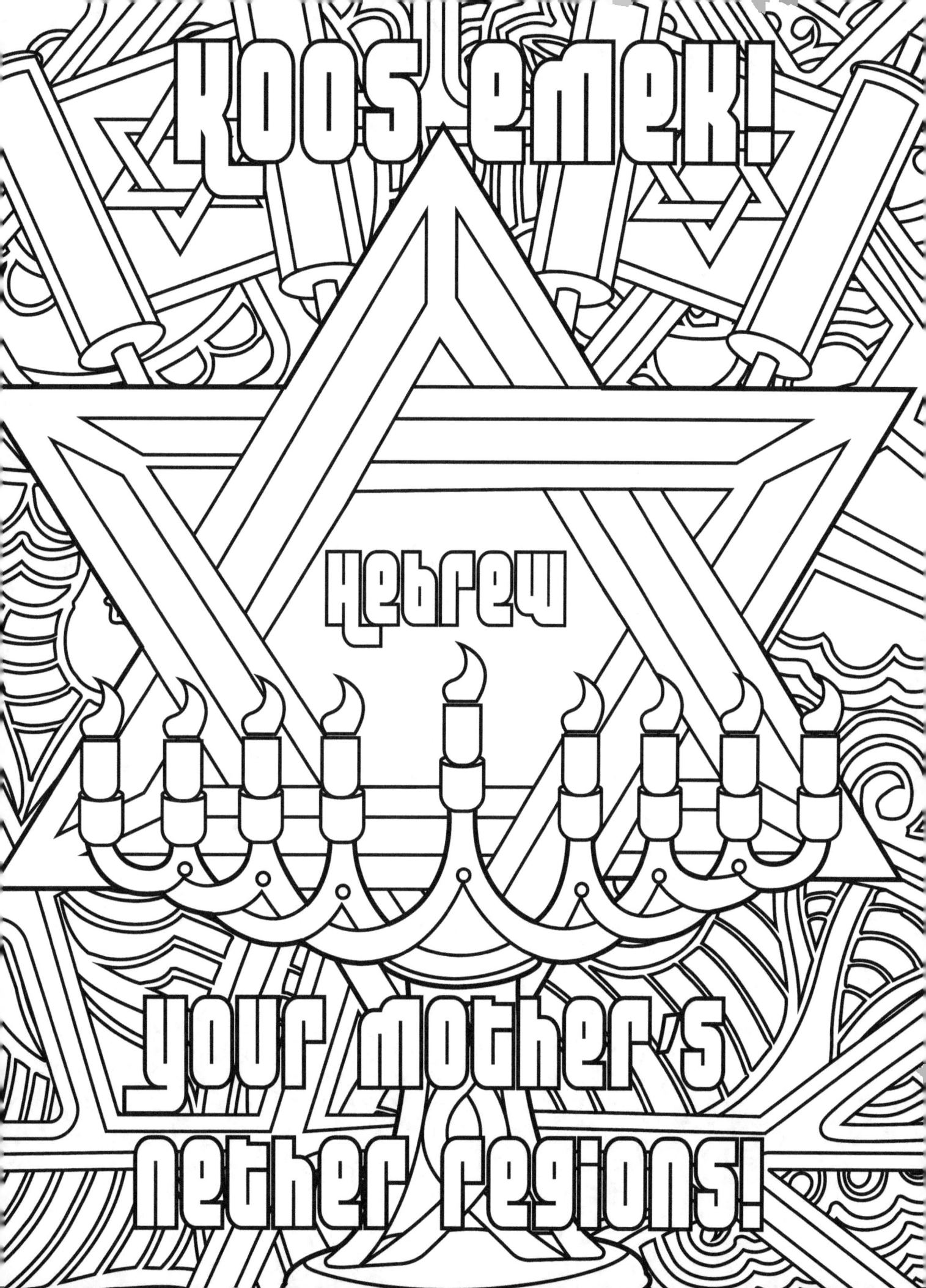

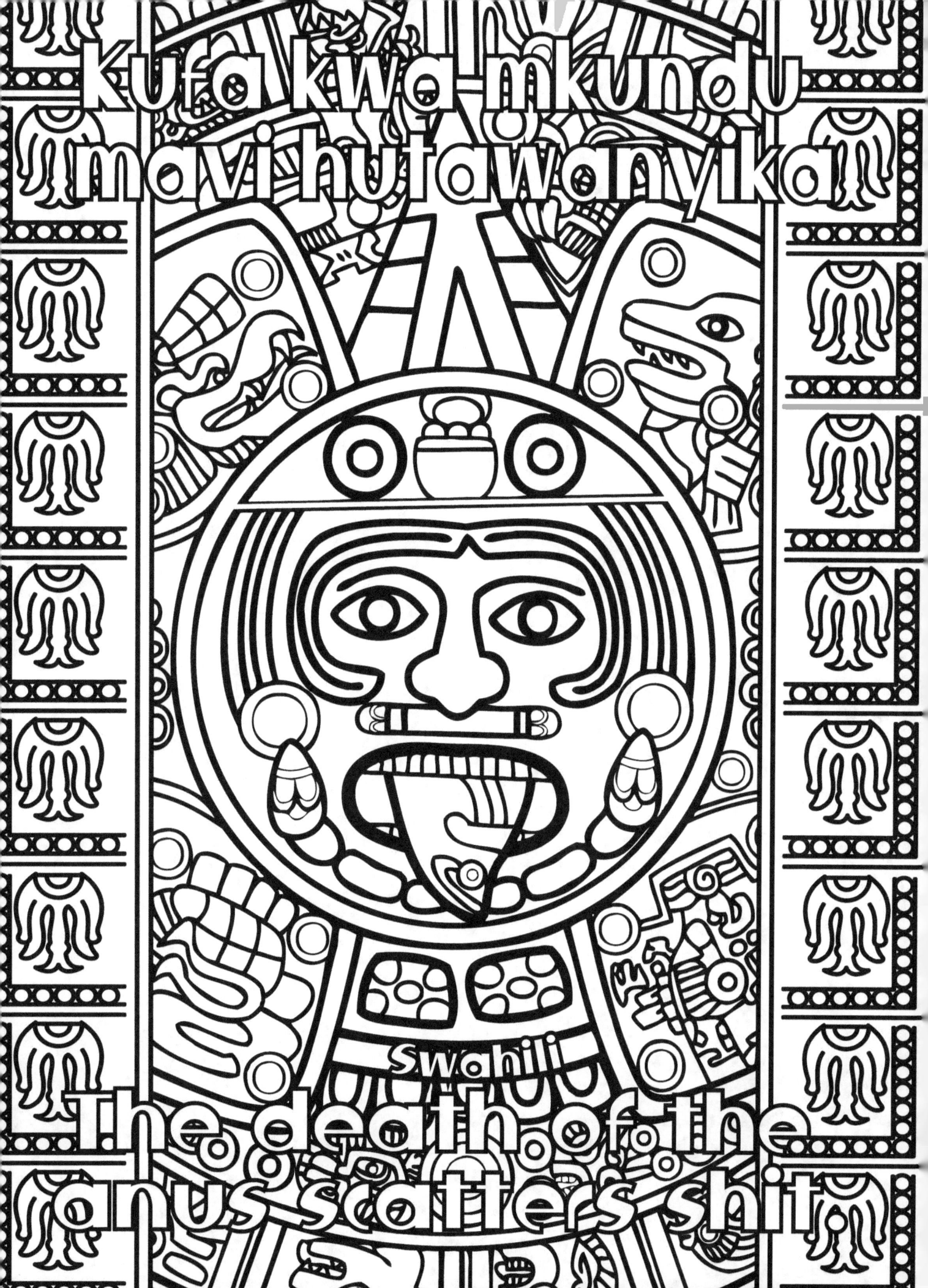

kufa kwa mkundu
mavi hutawanyika

Swahili

The death of the
anus scatters shit

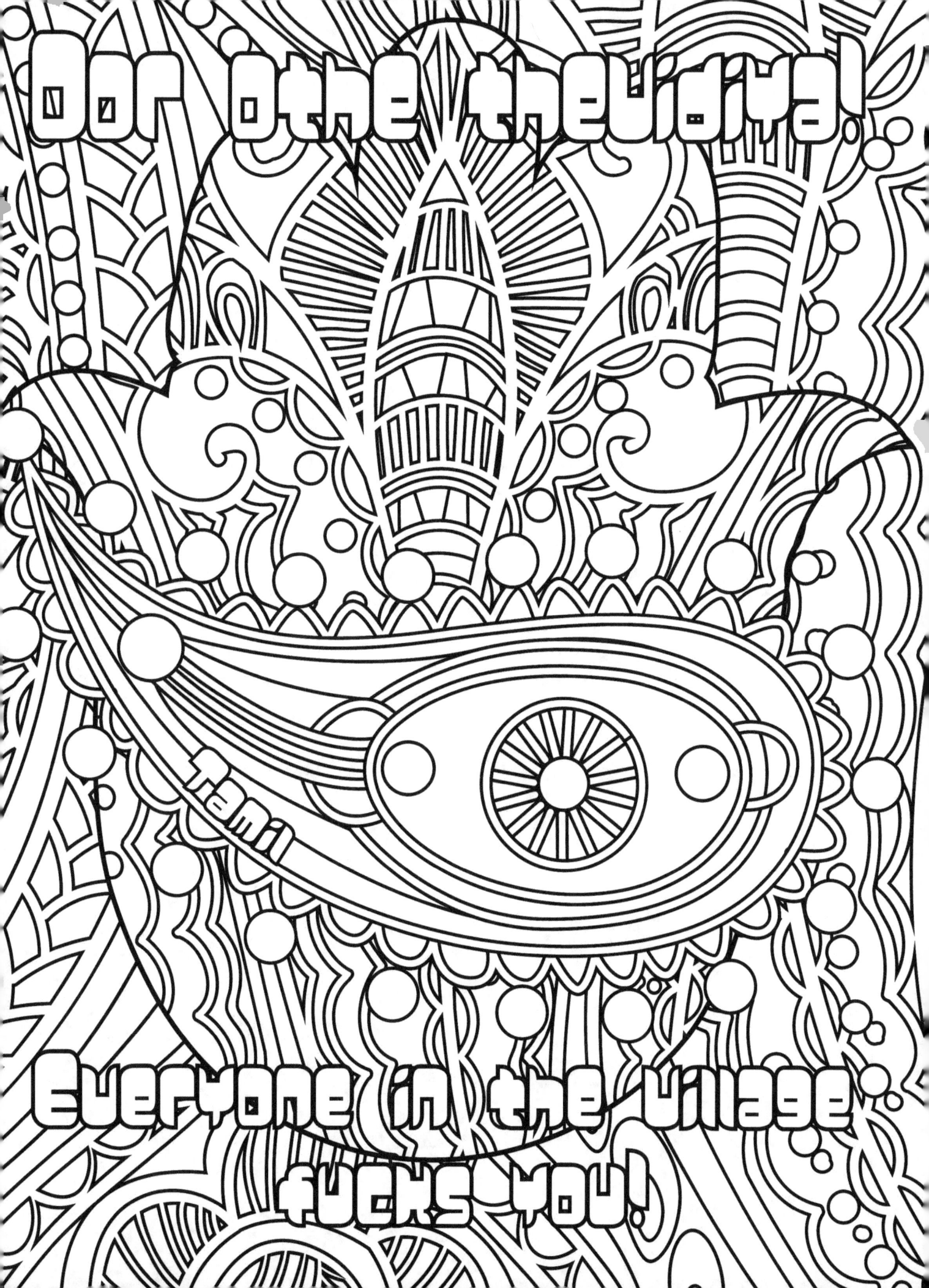

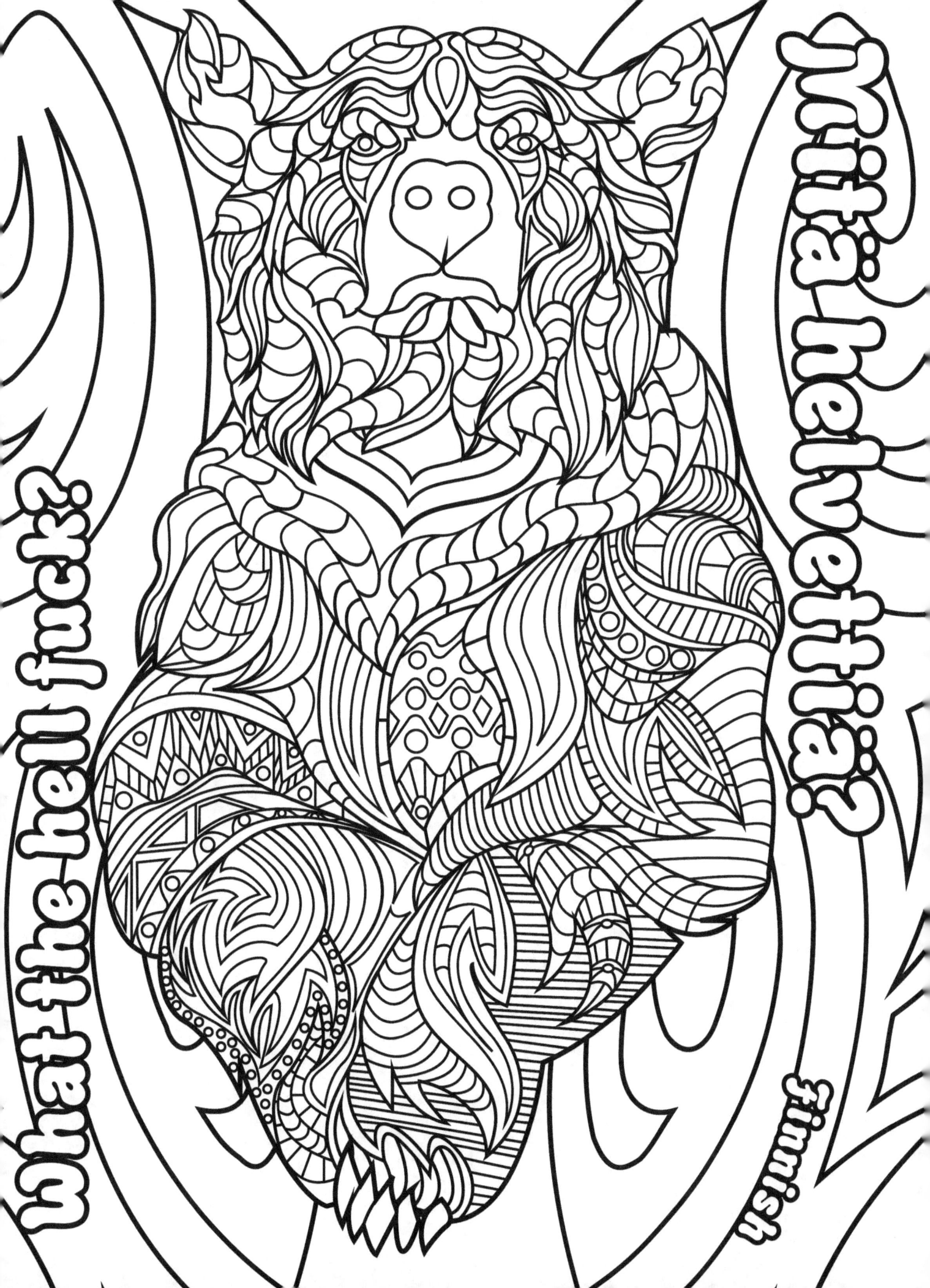

What the hell fuck?

Mitä helvettiä?

Finnish

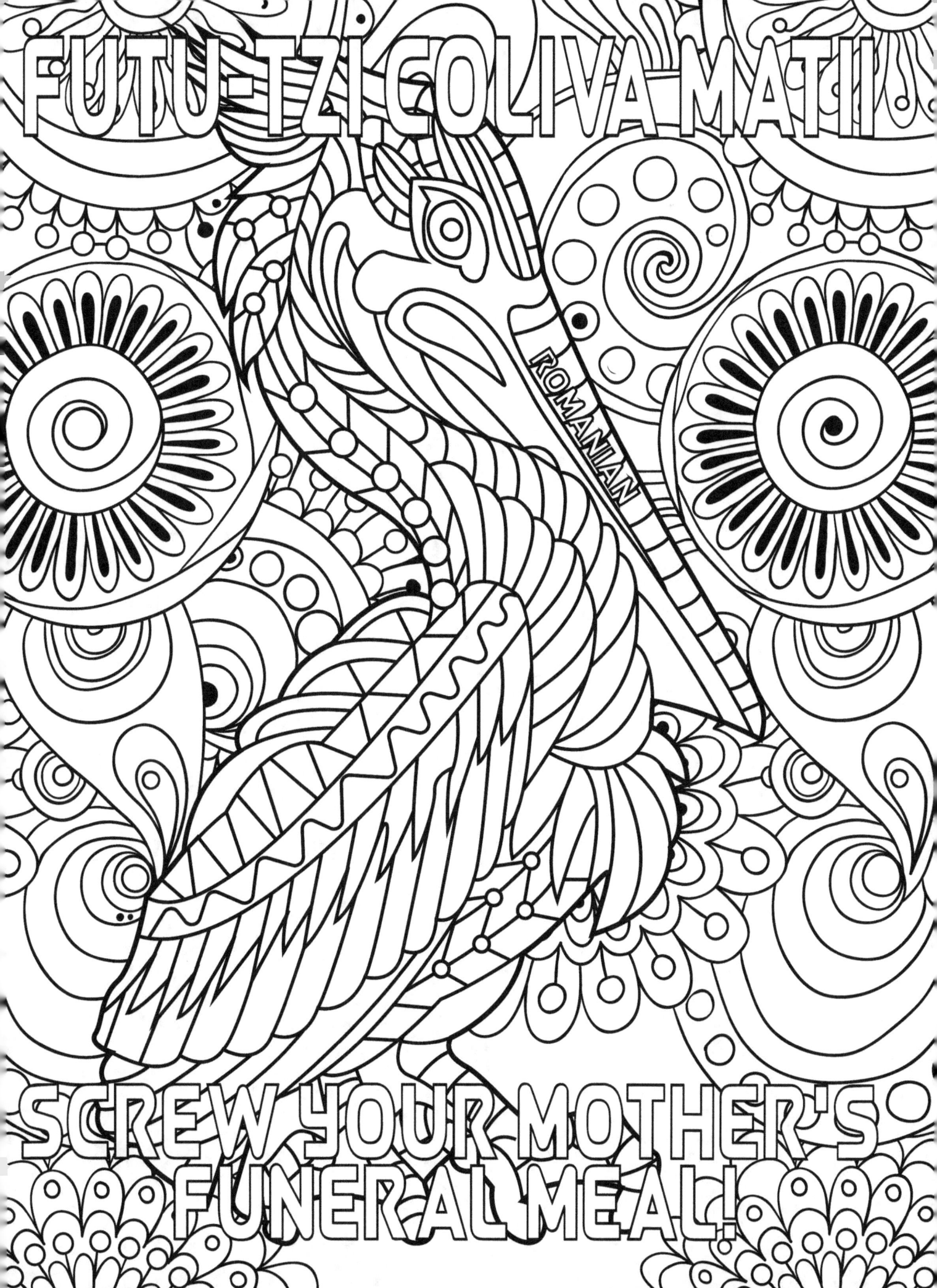

FUTU-TZI COLIVA MATII

ROMANIAN

SCREW YOUR MOTHER'S FUNERAL MEAL!

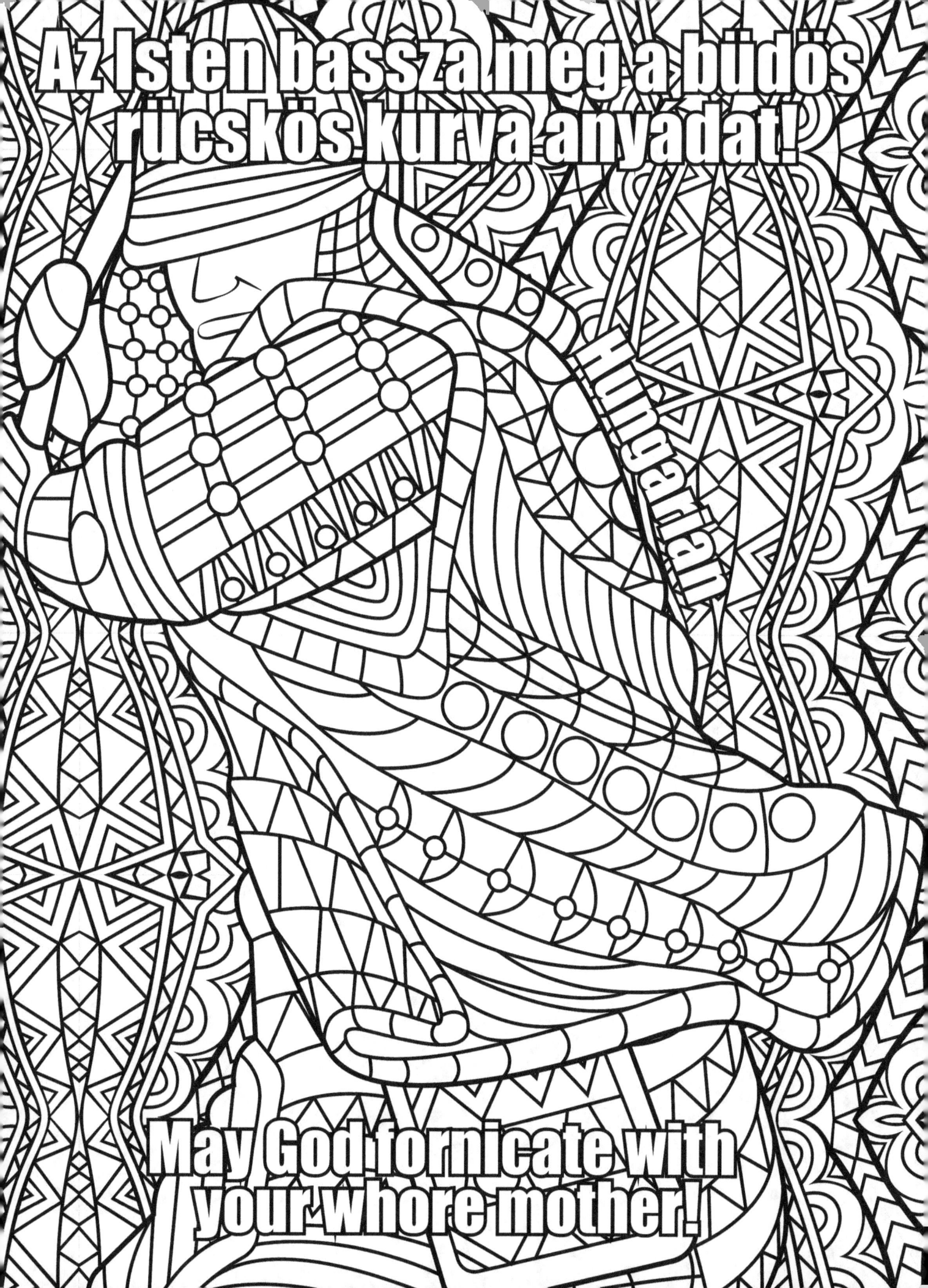

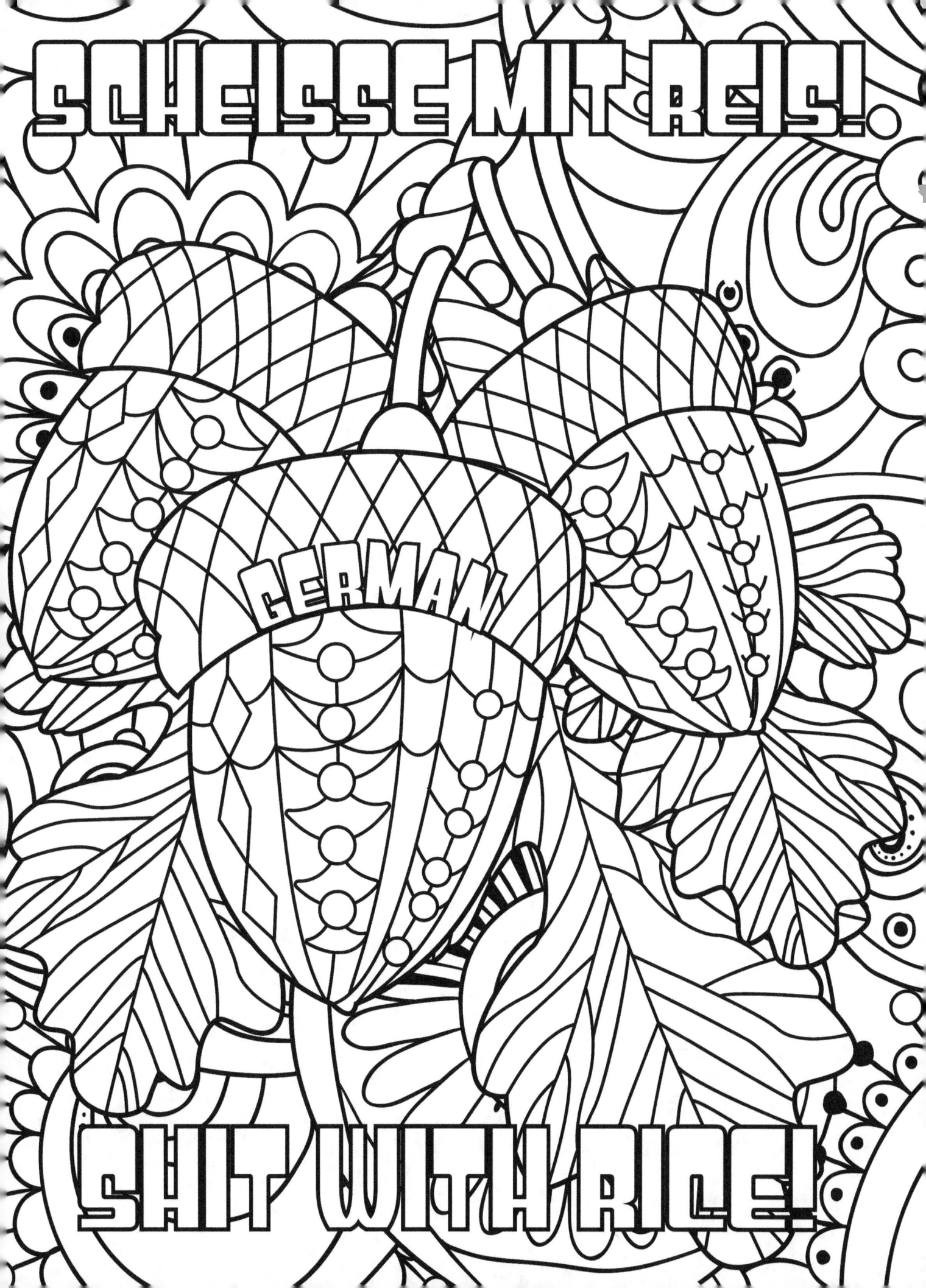

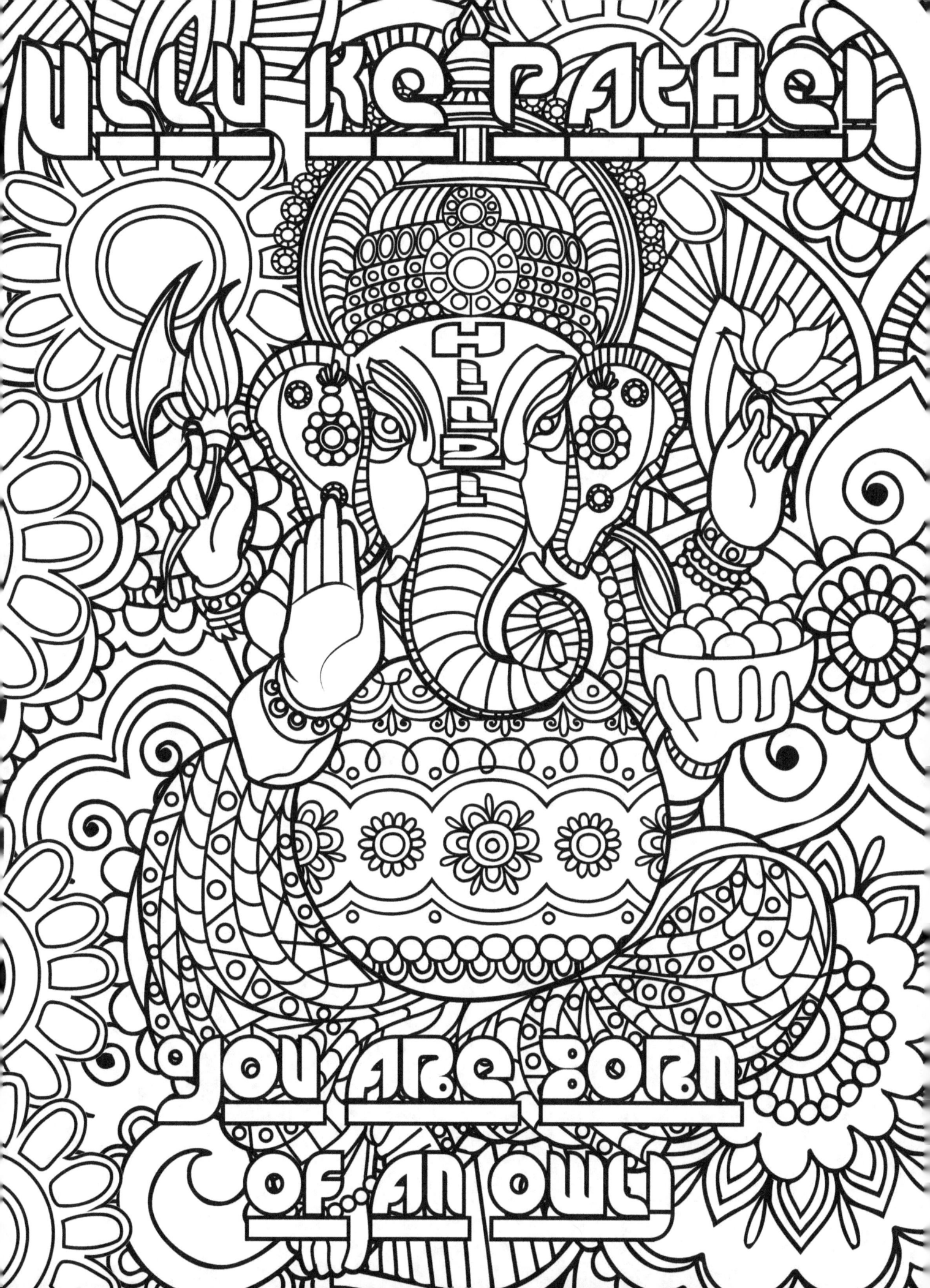

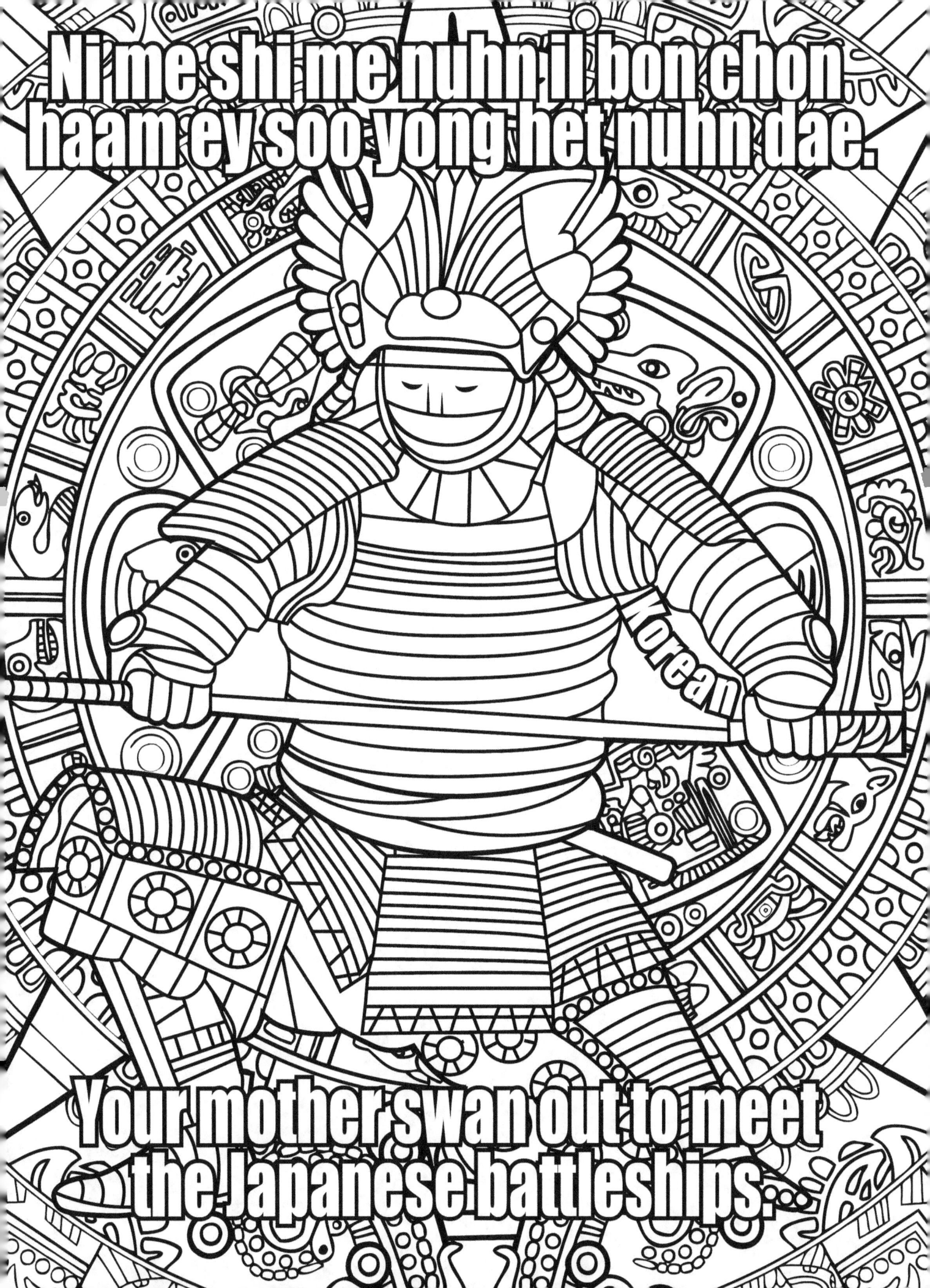

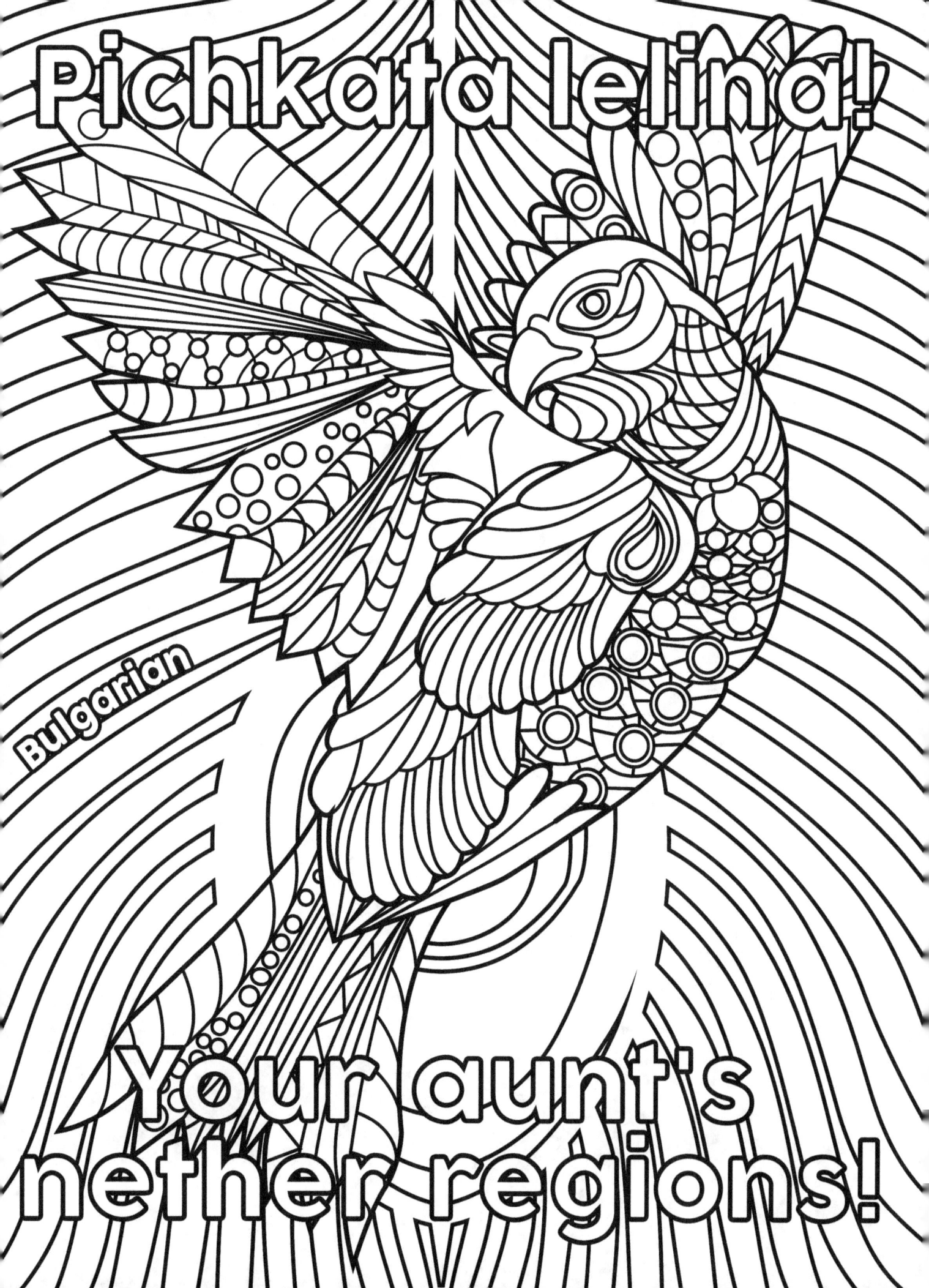

Pichkata lelina!

Bulgarian

Your aunt's nether regions!

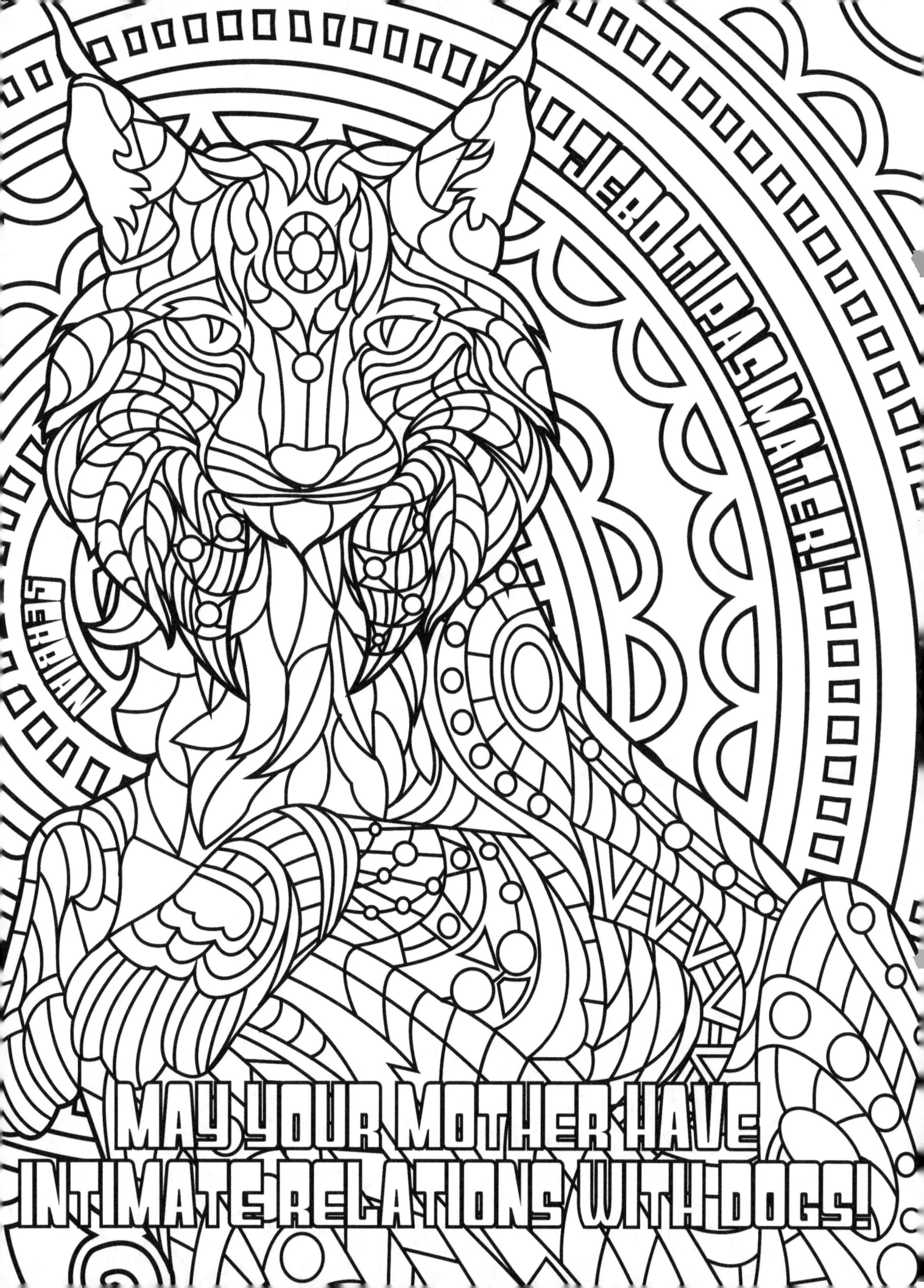

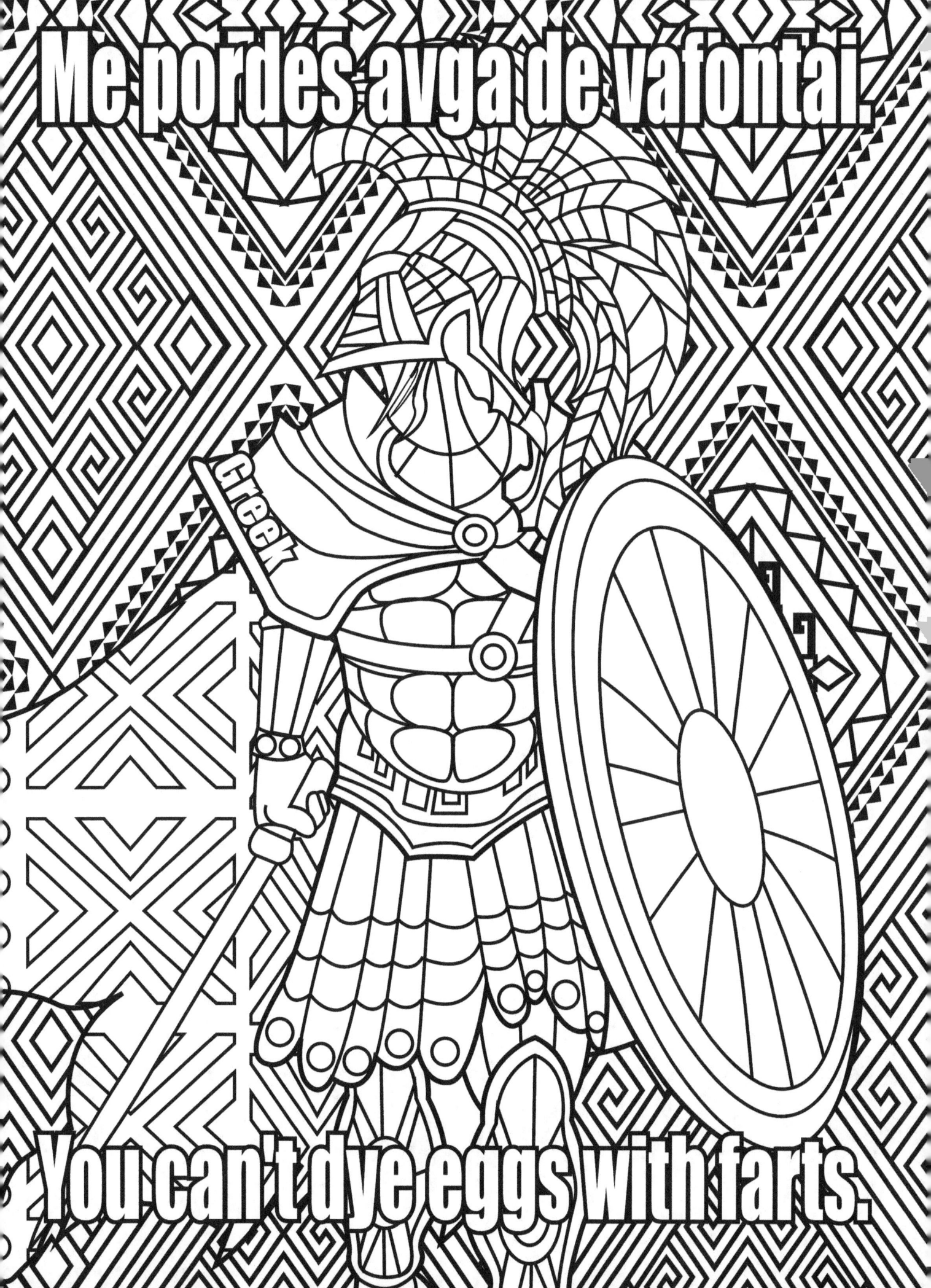

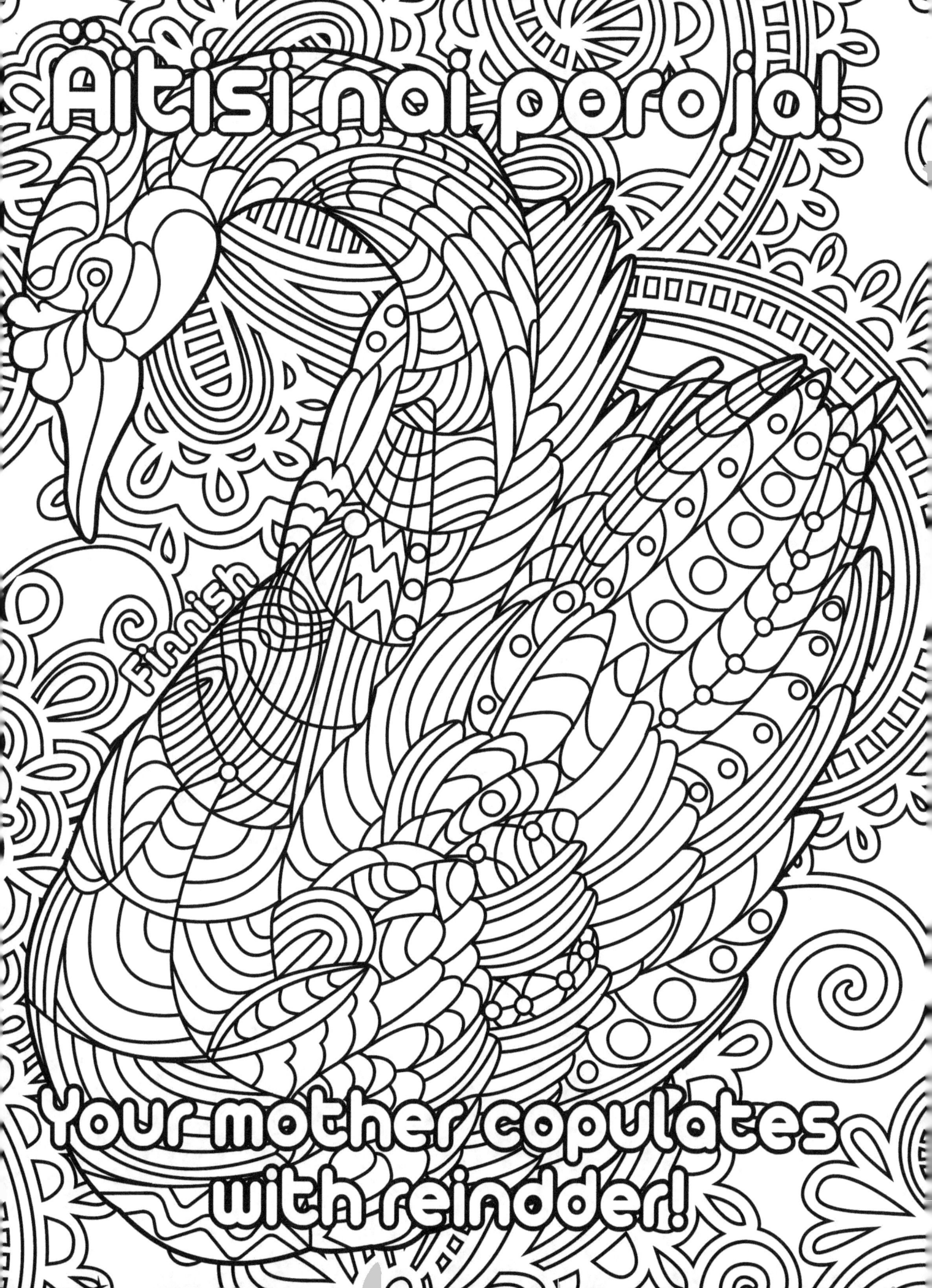

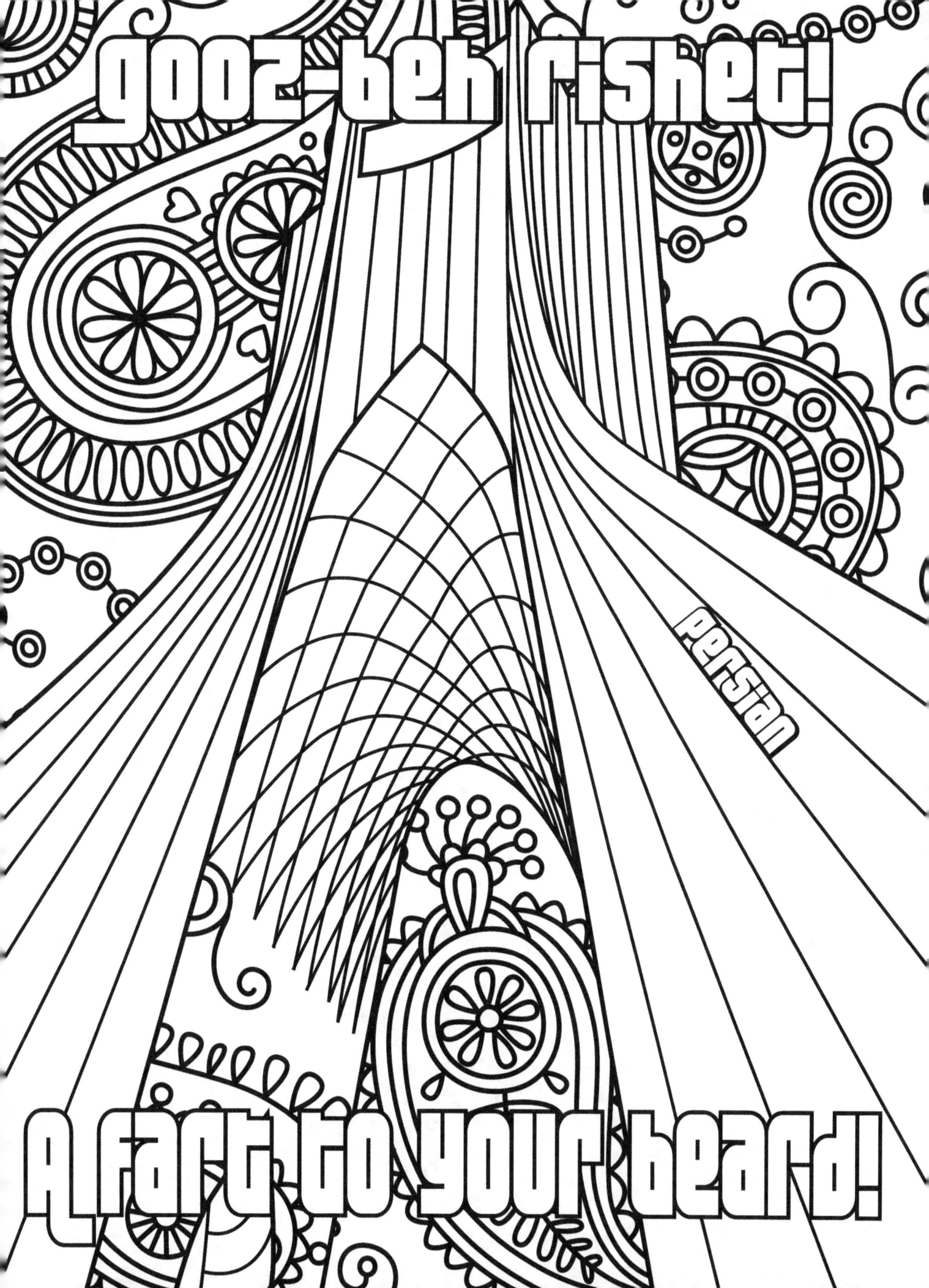

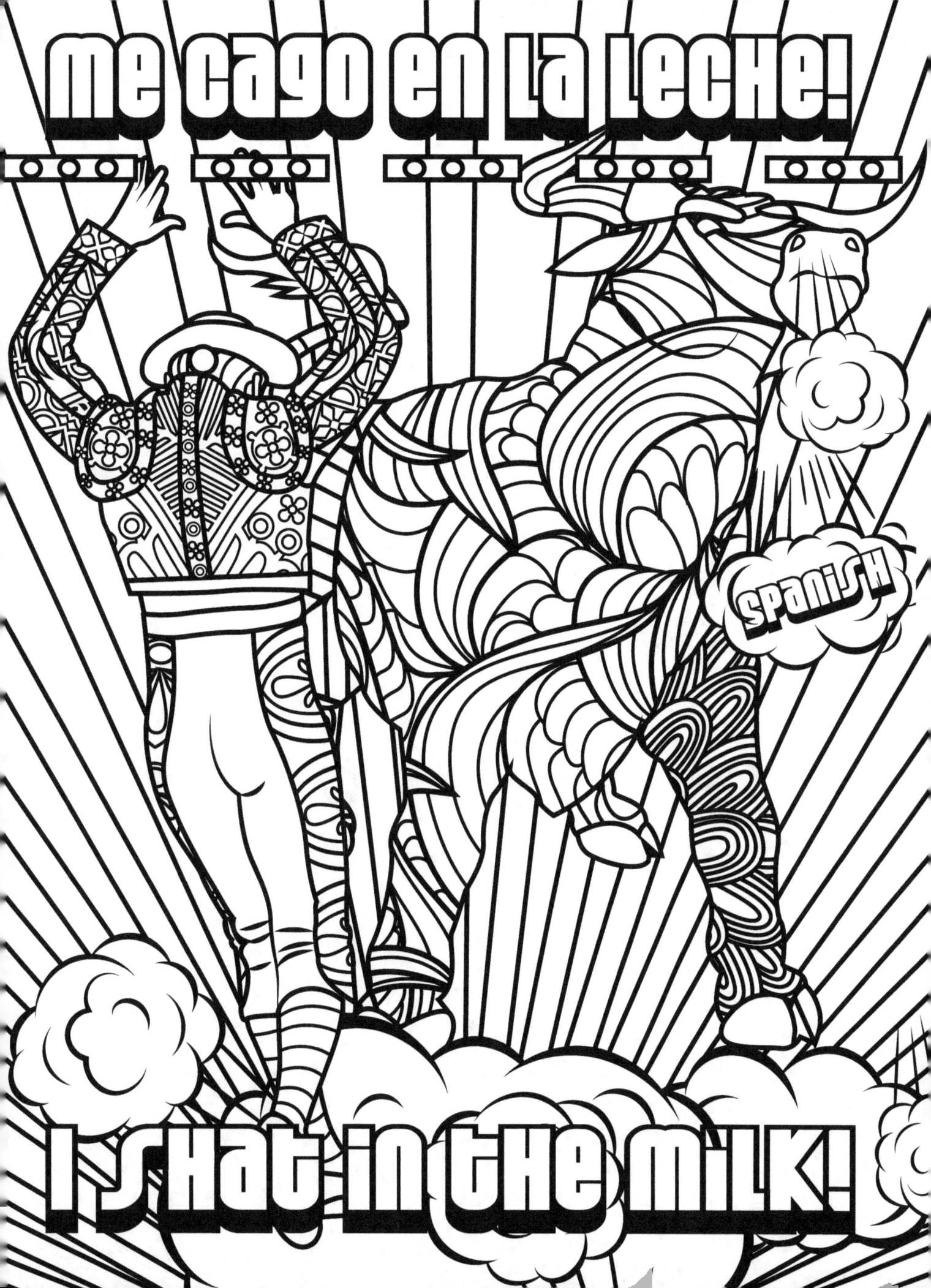

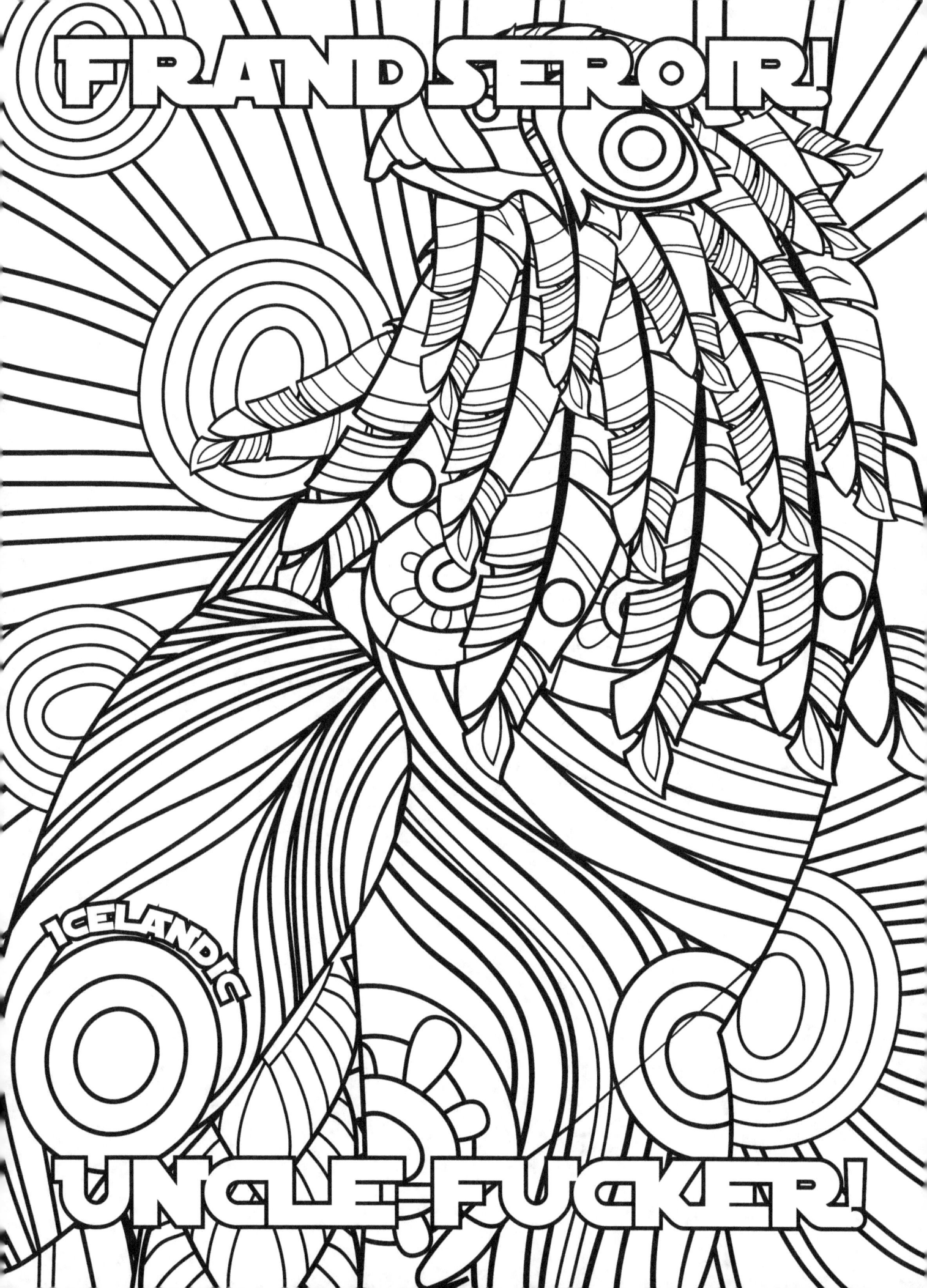

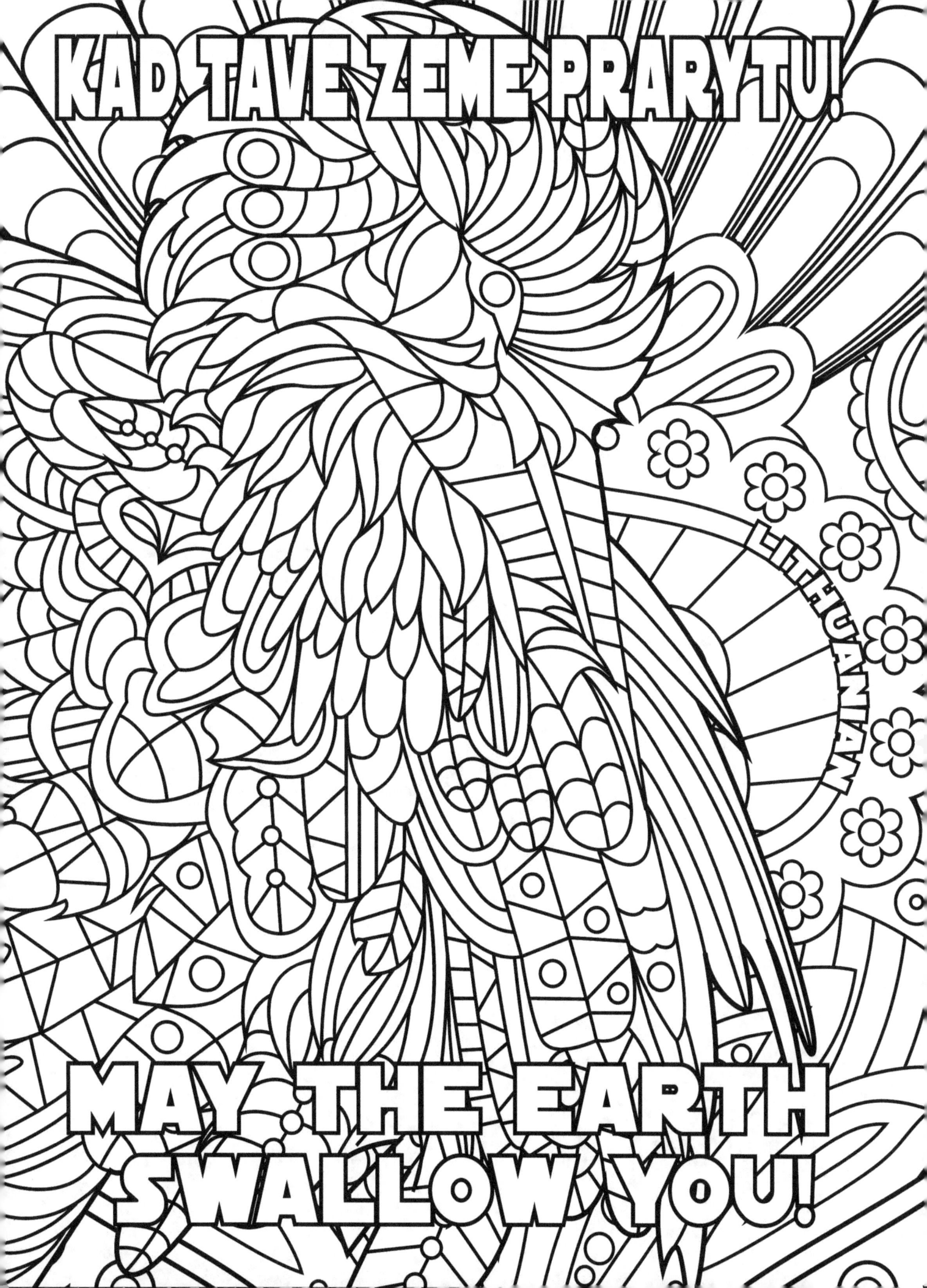

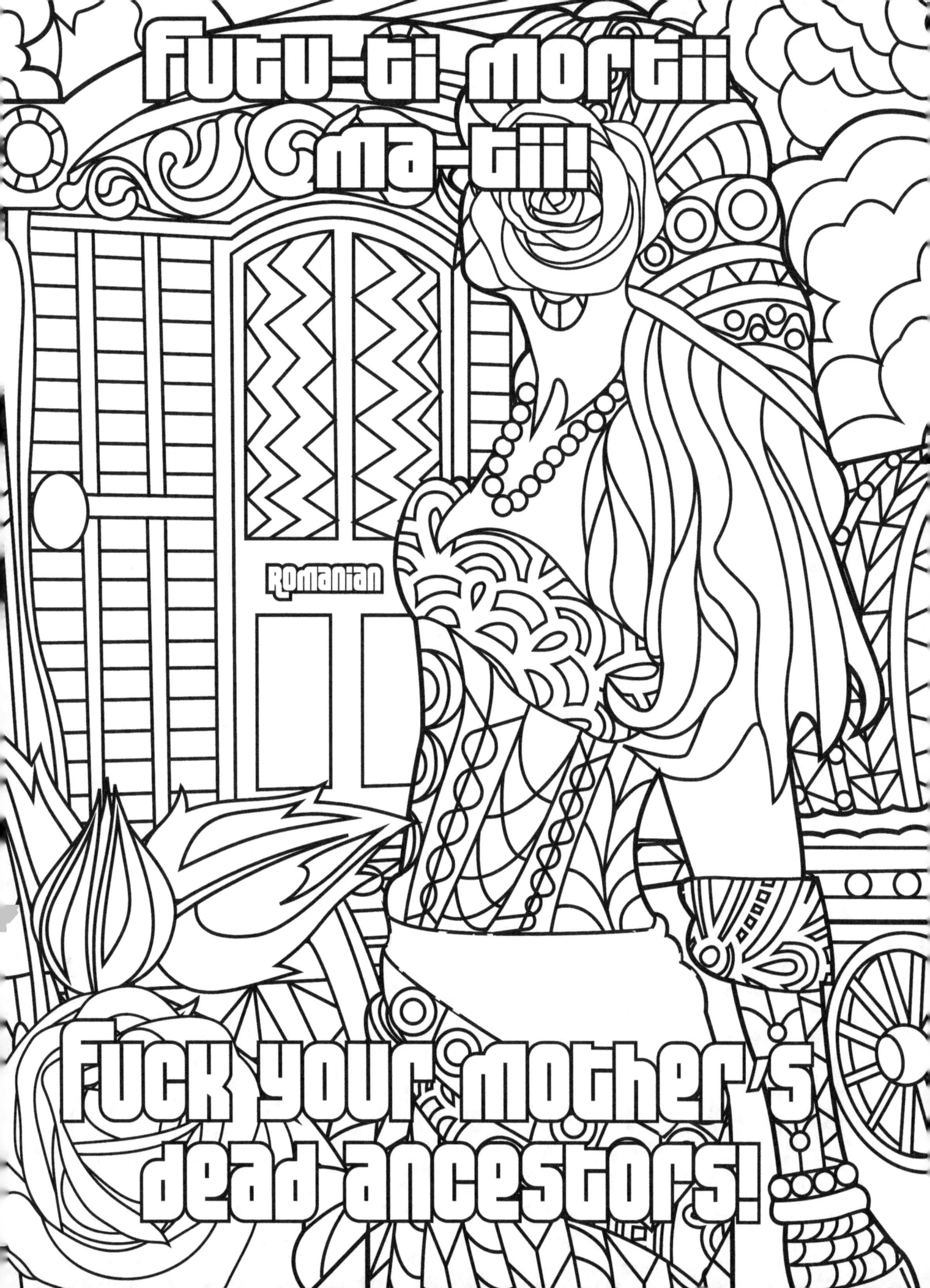

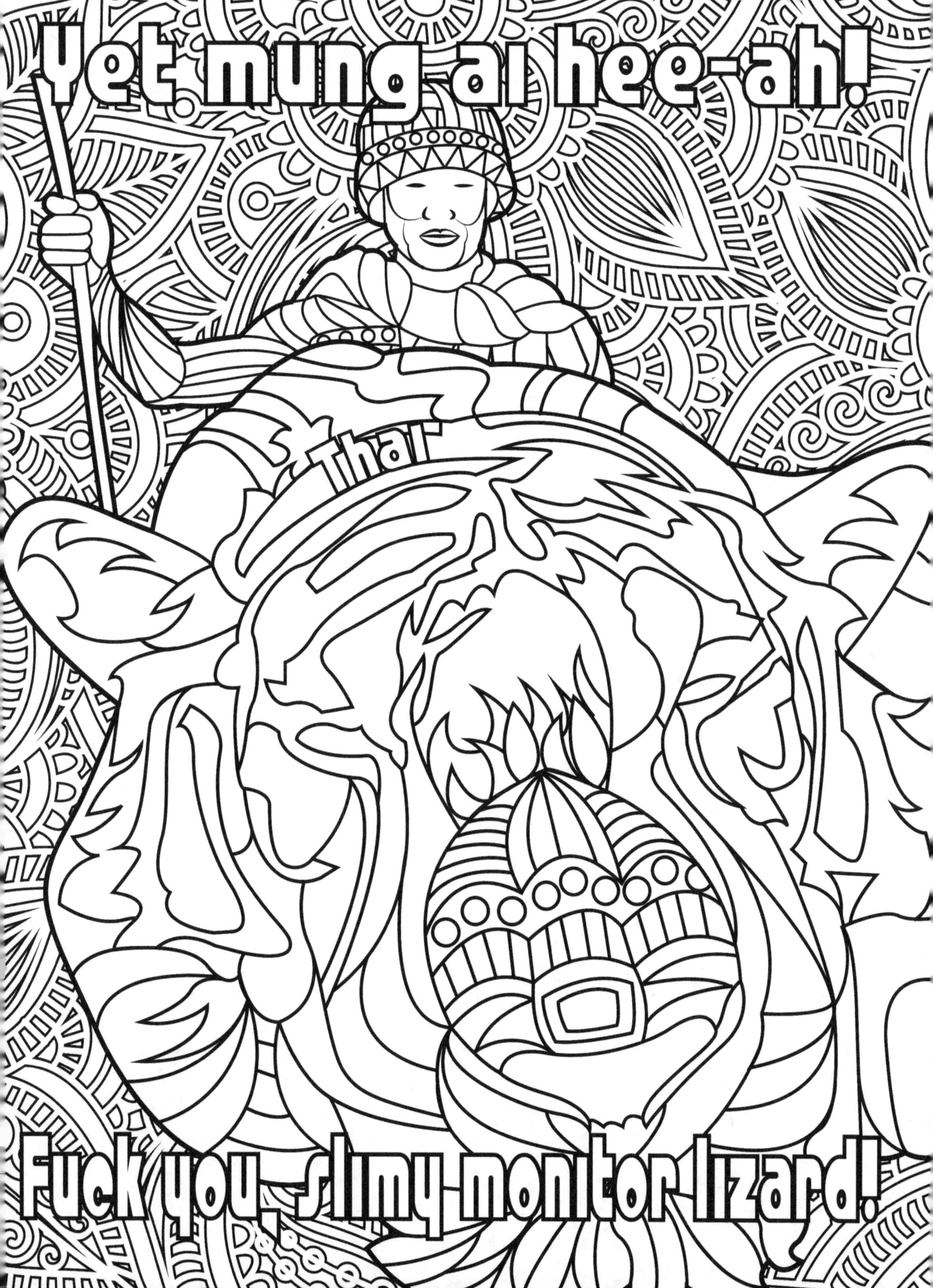

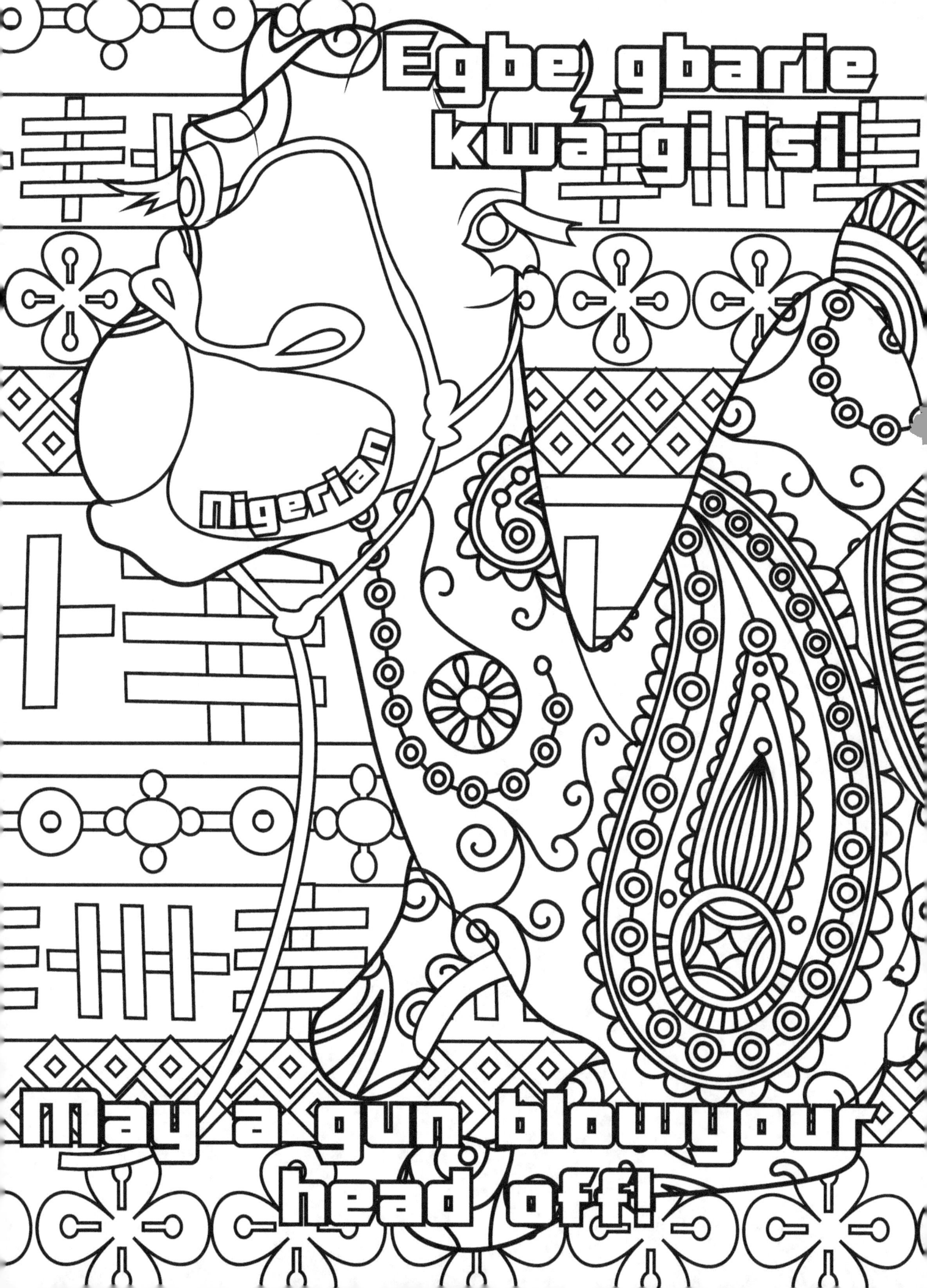

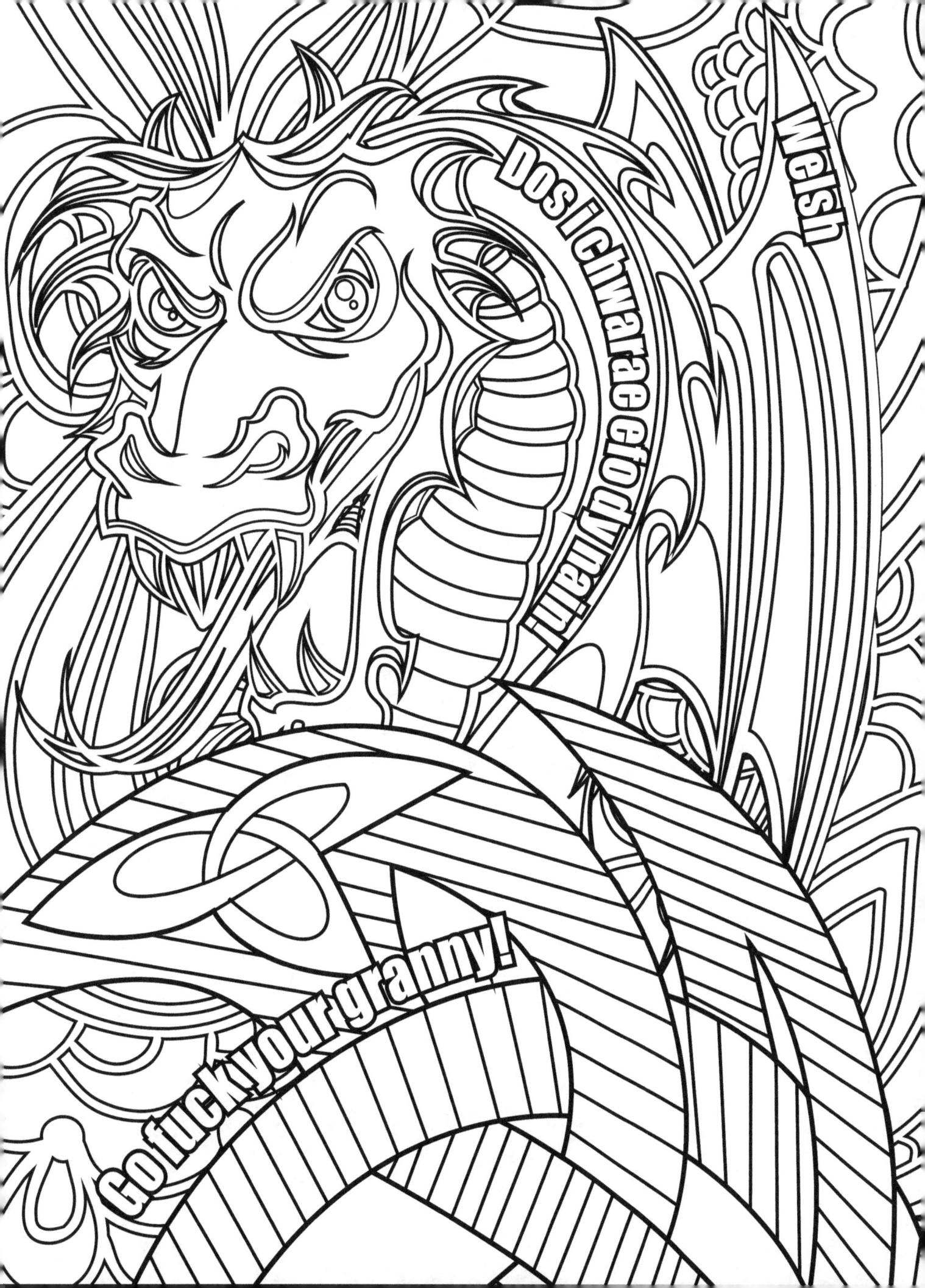

www.ingramcontent.com/pod-product-compliance
Lightning Source LLC
Chambersburg PA
CBHW081731170526

45167CB00009B/3777